KT-104-373

For Martha
    with best wishy

16 February 2000

The End of Finance

This volume develops an original critique of the belief that the present 'era of finance', where finance markets dominate contemporary capitalist economies, represents the best possible way of organising economic affairs. In fact, it is argued, the ensuing economic instability and inefficiency create the preconditions for the end of the dominance of finance.

The End of Finance develops a theory of capital market inflation rooted in the work of Veblen, Kalecki, Keynes and Minsky, demonstrating how it disinclines productive activity on the part of the firms, provides only short-term conditions that are propitious for privatization, and distorts monetary policy in the long term. The author examines the role of pension fund schemes and financial derivatives in transmitting capital market inflation and provides a nuanced analysis of the contradictory role they play in the financial system. Capital market inflation is also examined in its historical context and compared with past inflations, in particular the South Sea and Mississippi Bubbles, which spawned the first financial derivatives and the first privatizations. This broad historical vision allows us to see these forms of inflation as temporary and provisional in character.

A proper understanding of these complex phenomena, it is argued, depends on a critique of orthodox finance theory which merely extrapolates financial values from the past into a future of utopian equilibrium. The original theory of finance which grows out of this critique will be of interest to students and researchers of financial economics, practitioners in finance, and policy makers.

Jan Toporowski is Reader in Economics at South Bank University and is the author of *The Economics of Financial Markets and the 1987 Crash* (1993) and translator and editor of Michał Kalecki's *Selected Essays on Economic Planning* (1985).

Routledge Frontiers of Political Economy

The End of Finance

The theory of capital market
inflation, financial derivatives
and pension fund capitalism

Jan Toporowski

London and New York

First published 2000
by Routledge
11 New Fetter Lane, London EC4P 4EE

Simultaneously published in the USA and Canada
by Routledge
29 West 35th Street, New York, NY 10001

Routledge is an imprint of the Taylor and Francis Group

© 2000 Jan Toporowski

Typeset in Times by
Helen Skelton, London
Printed and bound in Great Britain by
Biddles Ltd, Guildford and King's Lynn

All rights reserved. No part of this book may be
reprinted or reproduced or utilised in any form or
by any electronic, mechanical, or other means,
now known or hereafter invented, including
photocopying and recording, or in any information
storage or retrieval system, without permission in
writing from the publishers.

British Library Cataloguing in Publication Data
A catalogue record for this book is available from
the British Library

Library of Congress Cataloging in Publication Data
Toporowski, Jan.
    The end of finance : capital market inflation,
  financial derivatives, and pension fund
  capitalism / Jan Toporowski
      p. cm – (Routledge frontiers of political
  economy ; 25)
  Includes bibliographical references and index.
  1. Capital market. 2. Derivative securities.
  3. Pension trusts.
  I. Title. II. Series
HG4523.T673 2000
332'.0414–dc21   99-12801
                                         CIP

ISBN 0–415–20881–5

For Anita and Miriam,
consolations past and present,
and a future without price.

BORKMAN: ... All the sources of power in this land – I wanted to make them subject to me. Everything that earth and fell and wood and sea contained and all their riches – I wanted to subdue it all and create a kingdom for myself and through it the well-being of many, many thousands of others ...

ELLA RENTHEIM: ... I joked about your schemes and asked whether you wanted to waken all the slumbering spirits of the gold.

BORKMAN: I remember that phrase. All the slumbering spirits of the gold.

ELLA RENTHEIM: But you didn't take it as a joke. You said 'Yes, yes, Ella, that's just what I do want.'

Act Two, Henrik Ibsen, 'John Gabriel Borkman',
in *The Master Builder and Other Plays*,
translated by Una Ellis-Fermor,
Harmondsworth, Penguin Books, 1958

Contents

List of illustrations

Tables

Figure

Foreword

This volume develops some of the ideas put forward in my earlier book, *The Economics of Financial Markets and the 1987 Crash*. Only after it was published did I realize that, for all its preoccupation with elucidating the 1987 Crash, I omitted to include in that book any general theory or explanation of stock market crashes in explicit terms. I therefore re-wrote Chapter 2 of that book into a separate article including in it an explanation of what causes securities markets to crash. This article, subsequently revised and extended, is the starting point for this book. The remaining two parts of the book are extended essays on funded pension schemes and financial derivatives. These show how capital market inflation, as described in Chapters 1 and 2, works in practice in the capitalist economies of our time.

While sharing a certain critical outlook on finance, this book is substantially different from my earlier book in four respects. First of all, there is implicit in the capital market inflation approach outlined in that book, a fundamental critique of the methodology that is commonly used in finance studies. This critique, together with an outline of my own approach to finance, is developed in the introduction below. Second, the analysis of how capital markets work has been extended in the first two chapters of this book. Third, this approach is now applied to studies of funded pension schemes and financial derivatives. Finally, my earlier book concluded with a moderately pessimistic view of capital market inflation continuing with underlying industrial stagnation. I had not then thought through the progressive character of Minsky's Ponzi finance analysis. This book now considers how capital market inflation ends.

An earlier version of the part on derivatives was published in *International Papers in Political Economy* (vol. 4, no. 2, 1997). I am grateful to the editors for permission to reproduce parts of that paper.

I owe a lot to those of my students at South Bank University who were interested in a more critical approach to finance. Much of this book was written with a view to providing them with something better than the normal finance diet of conjecture, mathematics and trivial observation. Jay Ginn deserves especial thanks for having asked me to explain the flaws of funded pension schemes. This gave rise to Part II of the book and the idea for the book as a whole. Philip Arestis, Peter Howells, William Luker, Randy Wray, Nina Shapiro, Tracy Mott, Larry Willmore and participants in discussions organized by the European Association for Evolutionary Political Economy and the Association for Social Economics, together with David Gowland and colleagues at the University of Derby, made helpful comments on earlier drafts of sections of this book. Malcolm Sawyer put forward some suggestions on a very rudimentary first draft of this book that have greatly improved it. Zvi Schloss kindly gave me the benefit of his extensive experience in the world of finance. Leslie Fishman generously gave me very useful advice and materials on Thorstein Veblen. Victoria Chick has been particularly helpful in encouraging me to think things through for myself. Her intellectual inspiration is further acknowledged in my introduction. Anita Prażmowska is owed very special thanks, and more, for her work in remedying the deficiencies in research support of my present employers. All this leaves me with the responsibility for any remaining errors in this book.

Introduction
Antecedents and methodology

The final decades of the twentieth century have seen the emergence of an era of finance that is the greatest since the 1890s and 1900s and, in terms of the values turned over in securities markets, the greatest era of finance in history. By 'era of finance' is meant a period of history in which finance prospers with such apparent brilliance that it takes over from the industrial entrepreneur the leading role in capitalist development. In this book finance is taken to mean capital or securities markets, as opposed to banking. It is very easy to forget at the turn of the century, when the world's economies are enchanted or bewitched (depending on the reader's point of view) by financial markets, that this leading role of finance has not been the normal state of affairs in the capitalist economies in the past. The South Sea and Mississippi Bubbles in 1720 brought capital markets into such disrepute that they played a peripheral role in company finance, although not government finance, until the railway stock boom of the 1860s. That era of finance ended in Europe with the First World War and in America with the Wall Street Crash of 1929. It was followed by a period of what is commonly called by enthusiasts for finance, 'financial repression'. That phase of financial history ended with the rise of Eurodollar markets in the 1960s, and the start of capital market deregulation in the 1970s.

In general, as Kindelberger has shown, an era of finance commences with an increase in the amount of money coming into capital markets.[1] This has the effect of raising prices, which then attracts more money into the market. The resulting capital market inflation has a number of consequences which are discussed in this book in the context of our present era of finance. Not least among them is that such inflation tantalizes society with what appears to be the secret of self-expanding wealth. In this way it bestows on the capital markets an apparently superior wisdom, a philosophy of effortless thrift which is held to be a proper guide to prudence and prosperity in commerce, industry and government.

With the rise of finance in the last half-century has come the emergence of finance as a separate subject of study and research: among those professionally engaged in finance and its regulation, banking qualifications, a knowledge of the relevant rules and legislation and a formal commitment to uphold them no longer prepare aspiring financiers for the complexities of their chosen work. In universities finance has moved out of the intellectual domain of economics and much more towards the financially more rewarding 'business and management' disciplines.

Its emancipation as an academic discipline has diminished the natural roots of finance in economics to arguably the most abstract and otherworldly axioms of pre-Keynesian micro-economics. According to these, markets revolve in utility-maximizing equilibrium with zero transactions costs and near perfect efficiency (except for governments which must sternly be held in check by various versions of the crowding-out doctrine); saving determines investment; and prices in general, and relative prices in particular, determine financial flows.

That the first of these axioms is fanciful is accepted even by the most eminent authors of theories based on such assumptions. To their great credit, even the most neo-classical finance theorists accept that financial markets in practice are very imperfect. However, they have not drawn the proper conclusion from this, namely that theory has to start from a consideration of the historical reality of markets, rather than assumptions about how they might work. This has important implications for the status of empirical research, which is diminished by being reduced to proving, or disproving, that markets may be like what theory suggests that they may be like. This point is further discussed below.

So attracted has economics become by the success of its offspring discipline, that the primacy of saving over investment is now disputed only by a handful of old-fashioned Keynesians and post-Keynesians of newer vintage. The so-called 'Washington consensus', named after the Washington-based institutions of the International Monetary Fund and the World Bank, which have done most to promote the view that the problems of all countries are due to their inadequate saving, has conquered the policy agenda in most countries. It provides the key policy justification for financing and supporting financial markets, modelled on those of the United States, throughout the world. The idea that increased saving is the precondition for increased investment, economic growth and human welfare has become a central ideological prop for capital market inflation.

One of the reasons why the primacy of saving over investment is an important issue of political economy is that it clearly supports the dominance of finance. Questioning it, as Keynesians and post-Keynesians have done, clearly leads to a denial of the dominant role of finance. Keynes, Kalecki, Steindl and their followers have argued that investment 'creates' its own saving. It is simply the residual between income and expenditure, while the finance of investment is conducted using *past* saving and current profits. Investment in production and technology therefore 'mobilizes' past saving and current profits, re-circulating them as income for suppliers of investment goods. This autonomy of investment removes the economic rationale for granting extraordinary privileges and veto powers over economic policy and enterprise to financial markets.

While Keynesians and post-Keynesians still argue their case over investment and saving, Part I of this book is devoted to the entirely new endeavour of controverting the third of these general suppositions. It puts forward the thesis that prices in securities markets are determined by financial inflows, rather than the other way around, and that, if this inflow is too great, it has untoward consequences for an economy dominated by finance. This view is then applied in critical examinations of the two aspects that appear to be the most distinctive features of this era of finance, namely mass-funded pension schemes and financial derivatives.

Anticipations of this view lie in the work of Thorstein Veblen, Rosa Luxemburg, John Maynard Keynes, Michał Kalecki, Josef Steindl and Hyman P. Minsky. Veblen advanced a criticism of classical political economy that in large measure applies to the pre-Keynesian neo-classical economics currently taught in economics textbooks: the rise of finance infuses virtually every transaction in the capitalist economy with a different significance and different consequences to those that such transactions may have in the barter economy which is the staple of classical and neoclassical economics.[2] In Chapters V, VI and VII of *The Theory of Business Enterprise* Veblen put forward a systematic and critical analysis of financial cycles that, in some aspects, has not been bettered in nearly a century since it was written.[3] In credit economies there was, he argued, a systematic tendency to the 'over-capitalization' of companies. Like Keynes and Galbraith after him, he argued that 'speculative prosperity' boosts stock prices in excess of 'the actual earning capacity of capital' and hence give rise to an eventual abrupt collapse in market values.[4] Veblen anticipated, like much else in passing, the adverse effect of labour flexibility on the saving habits of employees.[5] He was pessimistic about the possibility of regulating finance in such a way as to avoid disturbances to the real economy. Part of the reason for this lies in his distinction between managers who are 'engineers', with an interest in expanding the productive capabilities and output of companies, and the 'captains of finance' whose only interest is profit. By means of what Veblen called 'capitalistic sabotage', the captains of finance hold back production, relative to demand, in order to maximize profits.[6] Veblen's conviction that the 'engineers', who would nowadays be called technocrats, would overthrow the 'captains of finance' may seem, in the era of finance at the turn of the twentieth and twenty-first centuries, a miscalculation on a scale sufficient to condemn his whole analysis. But weeks after his death in 1929, the captains of finance in the United States overthrew themselves, plunging America and the world into the economic depression which was to be removed only by war and Keynesianism.

Such misjudgement of the future is an occupational hazard among economists, few of whom are as wrong as when they forecast with the greatest certainty. Without such misjudgements, there would be no need for any politics in political economy: everyone could just optimize in the way recommended to us by our textbooks. For the purposes of this book, Veblen's faults lie more in the way in which the financial institutions of his time have changed over the course of the twentieth century. Veblen did not look too deeply into the operations of what he called 'credit', which included securities. He did not separate out banking from capital markets, nor did he delve too deeply into the operations of those markets. His insistence that the value of a company's share (common stock) issue tends to equal its goodwill in retrospect obscures his argument. As befits the founder of the more sociological economics of American institutionalism, he was more concerned with how 'habits of thought' arise and affect business, than on how finance constrains those habits and the working out of this constraint in the economy.[7]

In 'International loans', Chapter 30 of her *Accumulation of Capital* written, like Veblen's *Theory of Business Enterprise*, in the era of finance that preceded the First World War, Rosa Luxemburg independently advanced the view that finance initially supports industrial investment, only to thwart it in the subsequent financial crisis of over-indebtedness.[8] Her analysis exposes features similar to those found in the crises of international finance experienced in the final decades of the twentieth century. However, Luxemburg saw finance as a relatively minor detail in her critique of Marx's scheme of extended reproduction, which came to overshadow her insights into international finance at the turn of the century.

Three decades later, in his *General Theory*, Keynes mounted his own systematic critique of capitalism dominated by financial markets. Chapter 12 in that book, on 'The state of long-term expectation', put forward a theory of financial value based on a conventional consensus arrived at in the markets and examined the precariousness of such evaluations. Keynes inferred from this his distinction between 'speculation' (anticipating the next consensus evaluation) and 'enterprise' (investing with a view to long-term income) and argued that the predominance of the former raised the cost of long-term investments. This formed the basis of his explanation of the 1930s depression. His conventional theory of capital markets and practical remarks on their limitations remain largely valid in today's much more inflated and technologically advanced markets. The American economist Irving Fisher advanced a rival explanation highlighting economic deflation due to excessive debt.[9] But he did not make explicit how the financial system brings about such excess.[10]

The life's work of Michał Kalecki was to reveal the secrets of the business cycle in the fluctuating financial condition of companies. The Principle of Increasing Risk, which he developed from the work of his colleague Marek Breit, argues that external finance, whether from capital markets in the form of equity or in the form of debt, is a liability for companies.[11] But he used this analysis to account for the size of firms and the course of the business cycle, rather than as a critical analysis of finance. Kalecki also developed our understanding of corporate profits as a macro-economic phenomenon, as opposed to the form in which it appears to businesspeople, as a mercantile excess of price over cost. He showed how gross aggregate profits (including depreciation) are a financial inflow that is determined by how much companies themselves invest, the government's fiscal deficit, the trade surplus and the balance between capitalists' consumption and workers' saving.[12] Like Keynes, he seems not to have been influenced in his analysis by the era of finance in the United States in the 1920s, when Europe languished under the shadow of war debts and successive German reparations crises.

Kalecki's former colleague Josef Steindl, in his *Maturity and Stagnation in American Capitalism*, written in 1954, first showed how buoyant capital markets may nevertheless result in under-investment by companies and later warned in general terms against capital market inflation.[13] More recent critics such as Paul Sweezy and Harry Magdoff have expanded on the contrast between the conspicuous prosperity of financial markets and increasing industrial backwardness in the most advanced capitalist economies.[14]

In a similar historical approach, Charles Kindelberger identifies a preoccupation with finance as a factor in the maturity and decline of capitalist economies without showing how this preoccupation arises out of inconsistencies in financial arrangements, and how these inconsistencies change in the process of capital market inflation that marks the hubris of finance.[15] Kindelberger's classic *Manias, Panics and Crashes* provides an effective taxonomy of the phases of financial crashes, with a 'displacement' in the real economy creating raised expectations and therefore arousing a credit boom. This is followed by 'euphoria' or 'overtrading', in which enhanced expectations of gain encourage speculative excess. Such excess naturally leads to the next phase of 'financial distress' when the swindles and the gap between over-optimistic expectations and the more pedestrian reality are revealed. The next phase of 'revulsion', in which investors try to get their money back out of the markets, naturally gives way to one of 'panic'. Here prices fall precipitately and asset markets break down unable to cope with the excess of sale orders.

In Kindelberger's analysis, and the more historical account of John Kenneth Galbraith in *The Great Crash 1929*, sentiments of greed, euphoria, frustrated expectations and panic, move capital markets in between an autonomous (indeed any unexpected) change in the economy, at the beginning, and the arrival of the central bank, as lender of last resort, to settle the panic at the end. It is true that expectations in financial markets are volatile, and may be more unstable than in other markets. The documentary evidence on this, from the earliest literature on capital markets, through Kindelberger's work to the financial press today, is quite convincing on this. But the mere coincidence of particular sentiments with phases of boom and bust in asset market may be just as much the *outcome* of those phases as their cause: with a fortune tied up in rapidly changing markets, a person would have to have a heart of stone to be unmoved by their fluctuations. Apparently more sober farmers and manufacturers of ice cream, bicycles and computers also make financial commitments in the face of an unknown future, and they may feel just as deeply about the trade cycles that affect their business but have fewer opportunities to excite these emotions in each other and articulate them in public.

While many small investors may be moved by sentiment, the large investors who move markets are inspired by much more strictly rational considerations. In a process of capital market inflation, reason and calculation show that the best returns are gained by adding to that inflation, even if prudence dictates that a contrarian tactic, selling while the boom is still active, is necessary to secure those returns. Furthermore, there has been an objective basis, which is more than just a 'displacement', in the capital market inflation of the last decades of the twentieth century. In *The Economics of Financial Markets and the 1987 Crash* I argued that trade imbalances have resulted in the accumulation of large financial surpluses which have inflated financial markets. In Part II of this book I detail how the proliferation of funded pension schemes is inflating capital markets.

The writer whose work is most immediately developed in this book is Hyman P. Minsky. Like Kalecki's analysis of business cycles, Minsky's notion of financial flows creating and recreating claims and liabilities which have to be serviced from the cash flows of economic units illuminates this author's own experience in financial markets as no other theories have done. Minsky's view that such financial 'structures' of claims and liabilities become fragile, and then unstable, broadly matches the course of the present era of finance, and previous ones before the First World War and during the 1920s.

Many financial economists, trained on a diet of financial modelling and econometrics, will find the analysis in these studies somewhat unsophisticated and lacking in 'rigour'. Lest they think that there are no methodological principles other than casual empiricism behind this analysis, it may be useful to explain the approach to the study of financial markets that is used here.

Victoria Chick and Jan Kregel have advanced the profound methodological insight that economic and financial theories are not abstract models but have, implicit in them, ways in which markets have operated in the past. The experience of past markets has not only formed the perceptions and 'abstract' ideas of practical men and economists. Those historical markets also contain in them the processes and mechanisms which brought about the results which financial theorists claim to be able to predict or explain by their theories.[16] Such real market mechanisms have tended to be obscured by nesting economic and finance theories in supportive *assumptions* about how markets work. The starting point of my analysis is the study of financial flows through the financial markets, showing where the money in those markets comes from, where it goes and what is the resulting structure of claims and liabilities. While most finance textbooks now have some introduction to flow of funds analysis, this is rarely linked to contractual financial claims and liabilities except in the case of maturity transformation by banks. The view that financial intermediation entails structures of claims and liabilities that require accommodating cash flows to keep them from collapse is Hyman Minsky's main and most original methodological innovation.

The examination of flows of funds and resulting structures of claims and liabilities has been accompanied by an intensive study of how financial markets work, the rules and conventions for trading and settlement, and the operations of firms in those markets. Much of this practical detail I acquired in my earlier work in fund management and banking, and this has been brought up to date by discussions with practitioners and extensive reading of the financial press. As a warning to those who research among pink broadsheets, business weeklies, brokers' and bankers' circulars and investment advice sheets, I should add that all this is not to be taken at its face value. The financial press has a very special function in modern financial markets. This is as an opinion board telling individual agents in the markets what average or conventional opinion is at any one time. Such an opinion board facilitates the emergence of a market consensus on market values. Somewhat less functionally, the financial media also operate to publicize trading intentions and history, which may or may not be true, but which particular financial firms use to find buyers for their schemes and securities. Such 'disinformation' has always played a part in financial markets since their earliest, shadiest, days. However, market authorities are reluctant, for understandable reasons, to admit openly that such market manipulation occurs, and most financial economists have been latterly prone to dismiss it as mere deviations from 'perfect' market structures and investor rationality. The study of the financial press therefore requires a considerable amount of searching out of hidden meanings and motivations behind publicly available information.

In this respect, the study of financial markets is similar to the art of Sovietology in the days of the Soviet Union: when a public pronouncement is made, or some stand is taken, it means that something is happening, but it is not necessarily that which is articulated in the pronouncements, or comments, of 'insiders'. In the Soviet Union this was because a particular vocabulary was being used to anticipate or 'form' the next political conjuncture. In financial markets it is because a particular vocabulary is being used to anticipate or 'form' the next financial conjuncture. In neither case are those making public statements necessarily liars or propagandists. It is simply that those statements have a different meaning to those operating in the markets, as opposed to those outside the markets. The function of market 'opinion' makes sentiment, at face value, a biased indicator of what is happening in the markets.

Market opinion and commentary are also partial views. The proper interpretation of events and commentary issued from the markets can only be obtained with an understanding of how the financial markets as a whole transform the flows of finance through them into future claims and obligations. Participants in those markets have to attend to the detail of events in those markets. Financial innovation and increased activity in the markets require participants to pay even more attention to the detail of even more events. In this situation less attention can be given to what is happening in the markets, as an integrated system of financial intermediation.[17]

The next stage in my research has consisted of thinking through systematically the more general implications of how financial markets actually operate. Their operations are examined in the context of the 'central problems', or key issues that those markets raise for the economy as a whole. The services that financial markets produce have no intrinsic use-value. Theirs is a 'use-value' that is derived from the functions that they perform for economic units outside the markets.[18] The 'central problems' of financial markets are therefore determined by problems in the way in which the markets function in the economy outside the markets, rather than internal 'imperfections' of those markets. Hence I would not regard the distinction commonly made between public and private information, or the issue of equilibrium in financial markets, as central problems. But I do consider capital market inflation to be just such a key problem because of its adverse consequences for enterprise, work, social welfare and public finances.

The final stage of my approach consists of describing the operations of financial markets in a way that shows how those market systems contribute to the problems so identified, and their implications for the wider economic issues raised. To economists devoted to formal reasoning and statistical analysis, this may appear as casual empiricism. However, I believe that it is if anything more rigorous than more formal methods because it requires full knowledge of how markets operate, which more formal and statistical methods do not require (and cannot handle), and reasoning about their problems.

Moreover, this concern for the systematic and problematic aspects of markets also distinguishes this study from the banal 'descriptiveness' that is the chief failing of casual empiricism. This analysis of the problems caused by financial flows through financial markets makes my conclusions much more real and vital than those of, for example, financial modellers. Linking the operations of financial markets, through financial flows and the creation of claims and liabilities, to capital market inflation and its effects on financial intermediaries, rentiers (savings institutions) and industrial capitalists, gives a rational and consistent explanation of the financial instability. By comparison, theories of price bubbles, market imperfections or collective irrationality that are narrowly focused on price movements in financial markets, or some isolated aspect of their participants' activities, seem faint, implausible and trivial explanations because, at best, these can only explore some feature of market operations. They cannot illuminate the apparent paradox of capitalism at the turn of the century, whereby financial innovation and growth lead incidentally to speculative industrial expansion, and systematically to economic stagnation and decline. Such a purpose requires a broader theoretical framework than is currently provided by conventional finance theory, which takes for granted the dominance of finance and therefore cannot perceive inflation of the capital markets.

The concentration of this approach on the way in which market mechanisms intermediate funds, and the clear predominance of statistical methods in finance, raises the question of the appropriateness of those methods to this study. Statistical analysis is a proper check on the arbitrariness and excessive abstraction of the axiomatic methods of reasoning.[19] However, this study of financial market mechanisms is more inductive and the examination of financial data comes much earlier in investigating those mechanisms. It would be tautologous to test the conclusions presented here on the data that contributed to them.[20] Those conclusions can only stand or fall by the consistency and realism with which they are argued, rather than their congruence with the data used to make them.

There are three reasons why I believe that statistics have to be examined in the context of the market operations which produce them. First of all, financial statistics are much less accurate than is widely realized. From the computer keyboard they can almost too easily be extracted and transformed into pristine continuous time series, ready for manipulation into functions and predicted series, in their turn ready for instant and increasingly complex correlation with other series. However, the original data from which financial time series are extracted are unreliable if not actually flawed. As indicated in Chapter 2, the fact that actual exchange of securities does not take place continuously means that the gaps between trades are made up using 'notional' prices advertised by brokers. This may not matter very much for the small core of 'blue chip' or most widely traded stocks or financial instruments. But even they may be affected by changes in the overall liquidity in the market, that occur over the course of business cycles. In a process of capital market inflation over an extended period more stocks become liquid. But this does not happen continuously or smoothly across all markets. As the financial crises of the 1990s have shown, even where there is a general inflation of the markets, switches between them may deprive some markets of liquidity and increase its scope in others.

When a stock or financial instrument is temporarily illiquid, the data used to make up a continuous price series is usually taken from the screen-based bid and offer prices of traders in the instrument.[21] Thus price data may not necessarily be representative of actual trades, but may reflect brokers' attempts to influence the market, or their own liquidity, or their subjective interpretation of other financial statistics as they are published. Brokers are not the only participants in the market who have an interest in influencing prices. Senior managers with stock options have a direct interest in the matter. When one has experienced at first hand the care with which senior managers and accountants manicure their balance sheets for consumption by the financial markets, one is less inclined to rely on the price data so influenced.[22] In any case, since the 1987 Crash, most stock markets have daily limits on price changes which suspend trading if prices move more than a certain percentage from their previous day's closing price. This kind of price constraint obviously invites manipulation since it offers a way of getting trade in a financial instrument stopped, as well as forcing committed market traders to keep price changes within limits if trade is to be sustained.[23]

Statistics on financial instruments also make inaccurate indicators because the functions of financial indicators change. Financial innovation and the rise of new markets changes the uses of apparently the same financial instruments. The process of capital market inflation also, and much more systematically, changes the functions of finance and financial instruments.[24] Even though such instruments retain the same name, and their value remains, for trading purposes, denominated in terms of the same money, their social and their financial value is altered when markets change. In the UK, for example, government stocks are sometimes used as a secure and remunerative temporary repository for funds, before investment funds decide how to invest them in stocks. However, now that the inter-bank market is a much more open market for short-term funds, in which non-bank, and even non-financial, companies operate, this function of government stocks depends on the yield curve (i.e., the difference between yield of long-term and short-term securities). Only if the yield of government bonds is greater than that available in the inter-bank market is such temporary holding of government stocks likely to take place. Since the yield curve changes over the period of business cycles,[25] this function of government stocks also changes. Apparently comparable price data therefore create a false impression of continuity in financial markets.[26]

The second reason for regarding statistical analysis as inappropriate for this study is that time series of financial data are always incomplete. There are strong reasons to believe that the recent past may produce misleading indicators of future developments. Hume's classic argument against empiricism, that the future may not be like the past, is well known. Since the 1970s, Paul Davidson has argued that because economies (and by implication financial markets) are 'non-ergodic', i.e., not having to hand universal data for all time, we cannot draw firm conclusions from fragmentary data of the past because we cannot reliably expect the future to be like the past.[27] Davidson's view may be modified with the observation that the reason why the past is not repeated in the future is because we learn and our social and material conditions change, so that we do not act in the same way as in the past. Because some of us learn, and because of our changing circumstances, history does not repeat itself, however much those who learn nothing from it may reiterate themselves.

Nevertheless, over time statistical data sets change as time series get longer, and more new statistics can be brought in from other markets. Hypotheses such as market efficiency, which were originally tested on US data, can now be tested on much longer series and are being applied to emerging markets, for example. If the volume of statistical data determined the reliability of statistical tests, then there would be a future in progressively more factually grounded analyses, as more such data becomes available. However, there is a third reason why this may not be so. Provisional results from statistical tests have their validity even further attenuated by the rapid pace of innovation in statistical techniques. In living memory, simple correlations and ordinary least squares methods have been replaced by Bayesian techniques, Variable Auto-Regression analysis, trace statistic cointegration tests, and Grainger causality tests. Supported by innovations in information technology, the high standing of quantitative techniques in the finance and economics professions, and investments in the improvement of such techniques, we can look forward to future revolutions in these methods. But this also means that even if there was available to hand universal financial data for all time, it would not be possible to draw reliable conclusions from it, because next year a more advanced statistical methodology may give a different result from the same data. The results of statistical tests are therefore always conditional on the tests used. At the end of time we may survey the results of all the tests, but by then any conclusion will not be very useful.[28]

Statistics therefore have to be examined in the context of market mechanisms if they are not to yield impermanent and misleading results from applying provisional techniques to inaccurate data. A fundamental methodological conclusion of this book is that changes in financing structures make past financial statistics poor indicators of actual market conditions. Extracting lasting conclusions from such data is more an act of faith than of science. This does not mean that statistics tell us nothing. But, like the information in the financial media, they have to be examined as a part of the market process, rather than an objective insight into that process.

The consideration of broader issues in finance makes this study a contribution to political economy. This is especially apparent in five aspects of the work. First of all, this study is rooted in an approach to economic activity that emphasizes the source of all income in the expenditures of economic agents and institutions, or what students of economics know as the circular flow of income. This was a feature of political economy from the first attempts at studying economic aggregates, in the work of François Quesnay. It was overthrown at the end of the last century by the Ricardian method of determining static equilibrium positions which are supposed to determine reality without being an observable part of it.

This study uses the circular flow of funds as the determinant of company profits. But it suggests the following important modification in the flow of income or funds analysis. When expenditures create incomes in the economy, the resulting financial flows do not entail any future liabilities or financial obligations: when a commodity is exchanged and paid for, all liabilities are extinguished in the course of the transaction. However, when the flow of funds is intermediated through credit or capital market institutions, future liabilities are created. As these liabilities accumulate, economic agents and institutions alter their behaviour in and reactions to particular market situations or conjunctures. As we have argued, financial parameters, such as interest rates, exchange rates and stock prices, acquire a different significance as financial markets are inflated. This book analyses how the present phase of capital market inflation affects the functioning of the economy.

Classical political economy also distinguished between economic agents according to the type of income that they receive. This traditional approach lasted until well into the twentieth century, and was even adopted by the founders of neo-classical economics, Menger, Marshall and Walras. The mathematization of economics and finance theory in the second half of the twentieth century, and their resulting abstraction and formalism has, as was noted above, obscured the social relations and institutions underlying financial and economic obligations and assets. Throughout the book the operations of three particular classes of agent are discussed. These are companies or entrepreneurs, rentiers or financial investors, and financial intermediaries (brokers or banks). All three earn their income from the returns that they make on their capital. This return is determined by claims secured against other agents in the financial system, relative to liabilities, rather than by the 'productivity' of that capital. The very different modes of operating of firms in these classes is discussed, in particular in Part III of this book, devoted to financial derivatives markets.

Third, the analysis integrates micro-economic aspects of economic activity with macro-economic aggregates in that it shows how decisions by economic agents influence financial flows between sectors not by mere summation, but by changing the balance of net outstanding claims and liabilities between sectors. The integration of macro-economic balances with micro-economic processes is a characteristic feature of, for example, Marxian political economy. There the key financial flow is the net inflow into the business sector, or profits, which determines that sector's financial and capital accumulation. This integrated approach pre-dates the twentieth-century textbook division of economics into separate macro-economic and micro-economic discourses, each with a different scope and methods of analysis.[29] In a modern economy with financial intermediation, these balances of net claims and liabilities have a strong influence on expenditures in the real economy, as well as on successive market conjunctures in the financial system.[30] This book examines the effect of such aggregate financial flows on the capital markets.

Fourth, this book offers a *critical* view of how financial markets function in the economy as a whole. Specifically, the consequences of finance for capital accumulation in the form of productive capital are examined here. The accumulation of capital is the distinctive characteristic of capitalism. It is that aspect of the modern firm which determines the nature and direction of all its activities, and the evolution of markets. Notwithstanding the motivations of those involved in these activities, in a capitalist economy firms trade in order to secure a return on their capital, and so that they can gain more capital. Capital markets offer new opportunities for capital accumulation. However, this is not an unambiguous benefit. In my earlier book I argued that capital market inflation depresses long-term productive investment while encouraging speculation.

Fifth, this book is a critique of policy towards financial markets. It criticizes the currently *laisser-faire* attitude towards capital markets, pension fund inflation and the regulation of financial derivatives. The book puts forward reasons why financial markets and capital flows need to be controlled. In Chapter 2, various ways of stabilizing capital markets are discussed. Relevant aspects of monetary policy are considered in Chapter 3. In Chapter 10, principles of financial regulation appropriate to the classes of economic agent operating in financial futures markets are discussed, from the standpoint of how the markets actually operate and their economic consequences, rather than the assumed benefits of free markets. Moreover, the regulation of capital markets implies social and political choices about social welfare provision and the claims of enterprise and finance on the proceeds of economic activity, rather than evading these choices with appeals to universal 'rationality'.

In Chapter 1 I show how capital markets modify the process of capital accumulation in two ways. First of all capital markets make the return on capital a liability that firms owe to rentiers in the capital market. That return is therefore no longer, as it was in the early years of capitalism, the firm's own internal financial accumulation (i.e., the saving of the excess of revenues over costs), which precedes actual capital accumulation through fixed capital investment. It is now returned or owed to the financial markets. Second, capital market inflation also inflates the liabilities of non-financial firms to capital markets. As prior claims on the financial resources of the firm, these liabilities then get in the way of accumulation through fixed capital investment.

The critical importance of capital accumulation in this analysis may also be contrasted with the conventional text-book analyses of the capitalist firm. The key concepts of this conventional wisdom are equilibrium rather than growth; the firm's autonomous determination of its own goals of profit or sales maximization and market strategy, rather than servicing its financial liabilities (headed by those owed to the capital markets); and harmonious optimization, in the sense of everyone's constrained utility maximization, with the financial markets setting the 'parameters' within which that optimization takes place. Recent history shows that the last of these assumptions is quite clearly wrong: the speed with which financial parameters have changed since 1970 would seem to imply a much greater economic instability than has actually occurred. Notwithstanding the greater *extremes* of recent business cycles, there is no evidence that they have become more frequent. The parameters have turned out to be much more unstable than the real economic 'equilibrium' which they are supposed to constrain.

The view put forward in this book is that financial parameters are a by-product of financial flows which may accommodate accumulation, but may also hinder it. This is explained in Chapter 2, which shows how prices in capital markets are determined by inflows into those markets. Capital market inflation results in the over-capitalization of companies. Since the non-government assets traded in securities markets are the liabilities of companies, the effect of this inflation is to reduce fixed capital investment. It is safer for over-capitalized companies to hold non-productive liquid assets against long-term liabilities than tie up funds in plant and machinery, the return on which is subject to the vagaries of the business cycle. The stock of other companies is an obvious liquid asset to hold, and trading in titles of ownership to companies leads to takeover (merger and acquisition) booms. Occasional outflows of funds cause capital markets to 'crash' or cease functioning. In this sense they become unstable and dependent on continuing inflation. Monetary policy, which is now widely regarded as the most effective form of government economic policy, is not really an effective way of stabilizing securities markets.

Part II of this book deals with the most important of the unique features of our present era of finance. As mentioned at the start of this introduction, an era of finance is marked by the domination by finance over industrial and commercial capital. The present era of finance is unusual in having finance, in its turn, dominated by funded pension schemes which have proliferated since the 1960s. These start off by placing large, but diminishing, funds into the capital markets. In this way securities markets have become temporarily inflated. But the funds also cause values to stop rising as the funds approach 'maturity' when they cease to inflate the markets, even before they start to realize assets to pay for their pension liabilities. To maintain stability, such a system needs to expand successively the scope of pension schemes in order to acquire more contributors.

Chapter 3 shows how capital market inflation creates an unstable Ponzi financing structure in securities markets, weakening real investment and the banking system. Chapter 4 considers one of the apparently unique features of the present inflation, namely the sale of government interests in commercial concerns, or privatization. This turns out to be not so unique and its precedents in the South Sea and Mississippi Company scandals of the eighteenth century are not encouraging. Chapter 5 introduces the notion of peripheral markets, i.e., securities markets which are weakly linked to large liquid savings institutions, and therefore are more dependent on the volatile affections of speculative investors. Investment funds inflate these markets by a form of emulatory competition while competing for returns in them. Chapter 6 examines the limitations of capital market inflation by pension funds. The decline of inflation, the relatively small proportion of the world's labour force that is in stable, well-paid employment, and rising unemployment and the casualization of labour, which will cause employees to hold their savings in more liquid forms, are all likely to reduce future inflows into capital markets. The result will be an illiquidity in the capital markets which will make stable withdrawals of funds from capital markets impossible. This will be a serious problem for pension funds and their beneficiaries in the next century.

Among the most prominent of these markets to have emerged in our present era of finance are financial derivatives markets. Part III is devoted to an examination of these markets and how they operate. Chapter 7 discusses the conventional means by which financial futures markets value instruments. Chapters 8 and 9 explain how rentiers, industrial and commercial companies and brokers or banks enter these markets with essentially different financial requirements, and therefore value derivatives instruments in different ways and are exposed to different risks. Trade in these markets is imperfectly competitive and may destabilize other financial markets. But financial futures markets are peripheral markets for the major investing institutions. They also play a marginal role in the corporate finance of non-financial companies, because liquidity preference is a more versatile and effective means of accommodating financial risks. Therefore the potential in financial futures markets for sudden disruption outside financial markets is limited.

The book concludes by pointing out the critical implications of the capital market inflation approach for finance and finance theory. First of all, capital market inflation is a consistent alternative explanation of financial asset values to theories rooted in either past values or some 'objective' productivity of underlying capital assets in perfectly competitive markets. Second, when capital market inflation falters, the practical object of the markets is no longer to serve as a facility for the rest of the economy, but to secure a renewed inflow. Economic development becomes only an incidental outcome of capital market operations. Finally, the analysis suggests that our era of finance may be coming to an end because of the increasing liabilities of funded pension schemes, the finite opportunities for expanding the scope of contributions to them, and the limited possibilities of replacing their capital market buying.

Part I
The theory of capital market inflation

1 Capital markets and the real economy

1.1 'Outside' finance and industry

Almost without exception, contemporary economic theory extols capital markets as the financiers and controlling mechanism of the capitalist system. The financial failures of government-owned enterprises and the less developed countries are commonly attributed to the absence of capital market constraints on their profligacy. This is epitomized in the standard textbook view of these markets:

> The buying and selling of existing stock is important in ensuring that quoted firms remain efficient and seek to maximize their profits ... The stock market encourages efficiency and profitability of firms and thereby benefits the economy in general ... A well-developed stock market with a high degree of liquidity therefore helps to both increase the volume of new issues and their costs ...
>
> The performance of the stock market also has both a direct wealth effect on expenditure decisions and also an important confidence influence on economic agents. As the real value of shares rises, the wealth and usually the confidence of economic agents is raised, this encourages greater expenditure and investment which can reduce unemployment and contributes to economic growth. If the stockmarket is performing poorly this tends to lower agents' wealth and confidence, and generally has an adverse impact on the economy.[1]

But the most cursory historical research reveals that capital markets have only recently taken up their present role of financing capitalist enterprise. The theorist who identified capitalism with the development of markets, Adam Smith, makes only incidental mention of capital markets, obviously because in his lifetime their existence was still tenuous.[2] He was, moreover, sceptical about the usefulness of the joint stock system arguing that, without exclusive monopolies, it was suitable only for financing operations that

> are capable of being reduced to what is called routine, or to such a uniformity of method as admits little or no variation. Of this kind is,

first, the banking trade; secondly the trade of insurance from fire and from seas risk, and capture in time of war; thirdly the trade of making and maintaining a navigable cut or canal; and, fourthly, the similar trade of bringing water for the supply of a great city.[3]

The main condition for the development of equity (common stock) markets, the joint stock system of company ownership, did not become legal for industrial companies in industrialized countries until the 1860s. Even then, the key actual function of the capital market was not the creation of a market that would allow capital to be switched between companies, but the tapping of the wealth of the old, principally landed, upper classes, in order to provide finance for the enterprises needed to establish the new capital-intensive industries of the second half of the nineteenth century: railways, shipbuilding and public utilities, such as Smith's water supply companies. In the British Empire and the Americas, this was done by the setting up of stock exchanges in which the wealthy were encouraged to keep their money capital, and through which trust companies and insurance funds invested long-term household savings. In this way, the problem of under-financing of entrepreneurs, first identified by the early nineteenth-century French utopian socialist thinker Claude Henri Saint-Simon, could be overcome.[4]

In the years that followed the 1860s, entrepreneurs refinanced their investments through those markets. However, where stock was issued to finance investment, for example in railways, this proved in general to be a highly speculative and frequently financially disastrous enterprise. In France and continental Europe, where a *crédit mobilier* system of banking developed under the influence of Saint-Simon's ideas, banks have tended to provide more flexible forms of finance.[5]

The emergence of the joint stock system in industry, whether mediated through stock markets or banks, altered the capitalist system in a fundamental way. Under the previous system of entrepreneurial capitalism, the owner of an enterprise committed his finances fully to that enterprise. In a recession, the owner had no means of withdrawing his capital and hence was forced to continue to finance his company for as long as he had money or there was a reasonable hope of recovery. By contrast, in the rentier capitalism that was the outcome of the joint stock system, the owners' risks are diversified. Through the capital market, those owners may more easily liquidate their interests in a company experiencing difficulties, providing there are buyers of their stock. If there are no buyers, then the shares are in effect suspended and the owners of such a company have to liquidate the company to retrieve their money. Thus the benefits of greater access to finance for companies that a capital market affords are offset to some degree by the weaker commitment of the owners to their enterprise.[6] This increases the risks attendant upon capital market financing of fixed capital investment, and is the reason why 'rational' entrepreneurs occasionally 'go private' by buying out their less committed shareholders.

The analysis in this chapter does not, on the whole, distinguish between equity (common stock) and bond markets. When equity is sold in a capital market, the commitment of its owners to the economic success of their companies is, as we shall argue, impermanent: a fictional remnant of entre-preneurial capitalism prior to the establishment of capital markets. New financial market instruments, such as perpetual floating rate bonds, have blurred the distinction between the two types of financial paper and such instruments are frequently treated by, for example, bank regulators as equiv-alent, or near equivalent, to equity (common stock). Moreover, the degree to which companies continued to pay dividends on their equity even when making a loss during the slump of the 1930s, and the economic recessions of the early 1980s and the early 1990s, confirms that modern corporations in effect regard the shares that they issue as a liability.

Already in the 1930s Keynes had noted with characteristically eloquent disapproval the tendency to treat all securities as *traded* commodities rather than a long-term commitment to the enterprises issuing those shares.[7] More recent moves towards centralized electronic share registration have been justified precisely on the grounds that this facilitates the rapid turnover of their ownership. Official bodies such as the UK's Greenbury Committee on corporate governance may echo Adam Smith in lamenting the decline of corporate ownership to the status of merely holding financial claims on companies.[8] But, in this respect, it has made corporate ownership indistin-guishable from a company's other financial liabilities.

For the two classes of capital market instruments to be fully equivalent, bonds need to have the facility to be 'rolled over' when they mature, making them effectively perpetual. Most financial centres are sufficiently efficient to allow companies this facility. Where they do not, or charge a punitive price for it, this of course makes common stocks less equivalent to bonds. But, such circumstances add to, rather than diminish, the capital market risks described below. Nevertheless, it is fairly realistic to assume that equity (common stock) bought and sold through capital markets is in practice, like bonds, a liability, albeit one on which a different pattern of payments is allowed.[9] From the point of view of non-financial companies, the crucial distinction in corporate finance is between the internal funds of the company, and external bank and capital market finance which creates a liability against the company.[10] In Part II, where the differences between the liquidity of equity (common stock) and that of bonds are examined more closely, it becomes apparent that these differences are more significant for investing institutions at times of capital market disintermediation than for industrial and commercial companies.

The link between companies and the capital markets in general (i.e., bond *and* equity markets), and the flow of finance into those markets, is the basis of capital market activity and values. The interaction of companies with the capital markets does not occur in any random way. Nor does it occur by means of arriving at a series of equilibrium positions in the capital markets that are determined by the productivity of real capital, as current finance theory maintains. In fact, this interaction depends on what the capital markets do for companies in the real economy, and what those companies do with the capital raised in those markets. These determine the flows of funds between the corporate sector and the capital markets. Such financial flows are the chief means by which the capital markets influence their listed companies.

Whereas neo-classical theory emphasizes the speed with which the price mechanism in capital markets operates to bring them (and by implication) the corporate sector into equilibrium, this chapter argues that in the real world capital markets are a factor that strains corporate sector finances and exacerbates disequilibrium in that sector. For this reason capital markets are used in practice to refinance the reserves and productive capital of companies, rather than as initial finance for new fixed capital investment. A consequence of this refinancing mechanism is that it causes extreme shifts in corporate liquidity over the period of the trade cycle.

1.2 Liquidity and capital markets

The conventional view is that the capital markets supply 'factor services' to the real economy, i.e., they collect up the savings of households and advance them to entrepreneurs as capital, in return for which entrepreneurs pay out of the operating profits of their companies dividends and interest to households in proportion to the capital advanced and the 'riskiness' of the enterprise.[11] An equilibrium is supposed to be achieved between the demand of entrepreneurs for finance and its supply by rentiers (holders of financial wealth) by some explicit, or implicit, auction of the finance available, in accordance with the market principles of supply and demand.[12]

However, in the process of actual financial intermediation no such auction actually takes place. Let us suppose that there is a new inflow of money into the capital market. This may be from a company taking over another company, and therefore purchasing the shares of the target company. It could also be from an individual financial investor with additional money (say from interest or dividend payments) which he wishes to invest in the capital market. He decides on the stock which he wishes to buy and instructs a broker on the purchase. But this money does not end up in the account of anyone raising finance on the stock market. It ends up in the account of a second financial investor who sold the first stock to the first investor. The second investor is then likely to use that money to buy another stock, from a third investor, who will then use the money to buy some third stock from a fourth investor. In the case of the money which a company might use to pay for a takeover, the shareholders of the target company will similarly find themselves with additional money, and less stock. They will therefore use that money to buy stock from a third set of stockholders.

In this way, the initial money inflow will circulate around the capital market until it is taken out by a final investor, or rentier, who wishes to use the money for some other purpose (say buying a holiday home), or by the government issuing a bond, or by a company issuing a stock or share. Market intermediaries, such as brokers or 'market-makers' have the function of balancing the potentially inconsistent sale and purchase orders of these investors with accommodating sales and purchases of their own stocks. An obvious feature of such financial circulation is that there is no 'equilibrium'. Exchange continues until the liquidity put into the market is taken out or, if the initial transaction was a sale, until the money taken out of the market is replaced by a buyer putting liquidity into the market.

Even if the initial money inflow is eventually taken out by an industrial company, there is no auction mechanism to ensure that the funds obtained are applied to the most profitable projects in the real economy. The issue of new stock (the so-called primary market) is separated from the initial money inflow in time and in place by the many intermediary portfolio switches that eventually bring the money inflow to the company. The price or yield at which new stock may be issued, which we call the effective price,[13] may depend on the liquidity of the market at the time of issue, but it is not likely to be applied in practice as a minimum required return on new industrial or commercial investment. Most stocks are issued to replace other stocks or debt. Others are used to replace the internal liquidity of companies, that has already been used up either in capital investment or, in a period of capital market inflation, on corporate restructuring (mergers and acquisitions). The yield or price of a new stock is in practice the price of internal liquidity, rather than the opportunity cost of fixed capital investment, whose return in any case varies over the business cycle. The remainder of this chapter examines the reasons why companies prefer to use finance to manage liquidity rather than to buy additional productive capacity.

According to the most common view of finance, entrepreneurs are supposed to take the money put into the capital market and employ it in their business, as a 'factor', like land or labour, to generate sales revenue.[14] More specifically, entrepreneurs are supposed to use it to meet occasional working capital shortfalls or to purchase premises, plant and equipment ('fixed' capital). In this way, finance capital is supposed, by its own productivity, to generate additional profits.[15]

However, in business, working capital is usually more conveniently financed by bank short-term loans or overdraft facilities, or even bills and letters of credit. As for fixed capital investment, capital markets are inappropriate sources of finance for two principal reasons.

First of all, capital markets are inherently unstable, alternating between periods of liquidity in 'bull' markets when finance for enterprise is easily – perhaps too easily – raised and periods of illiquidity, when financiers tend to be over-cautious about advancing medium- and long-term funds for industrial and commercial enterprises. Broadly speaking, the liquidity of a long-term asset is the availability of a purchaser for it at a more than nominal price.[16] Whereas bonds have an assured 'residual' liquidity when they are repaid, in the markets for equity or common stock the liquidity of stocks varies in proportion to the rate of change of securities prices. When equity prices are rising, there are plenty of buyers and sellers around wishing to cash in on capital gains. However, when prices are falling, buyers are more likely to seek alternative, more promising investments. Some sellers may become reluctant to realize losses on their investment, but even those wanting to avoid further losses by getting out of the market are likely to become 'locked into' their investment by an absence of buyers. In this way, the normal price mechanism that brings into equilibrium supply with demand breaks down because falling prices cause buyers to flee the market rather than stimulating their demand.

Capital markets normally fluctuate between this liquidity and illiquidity in association with the trade cycle. The markets are therefore likely to over-capitalize a company in a boom and they can shut off the flow of capital funds to that company in a recession. These swings between liquidity and illiquidity may be exacerbated by changes in monetary policy over the business cycle (see Chapter 3, section 3.2).

This has a crucial bearing on a company's finances and any fixed capital investment programme that it may undertake. Such investment requires stable and assured finance. Over-capitalization will tend to leave a company with large financing costs, and the prospect of difficulties in meeting those costs out of its cash flow when the boom turns into recession. Although the issue of capital market instruments raises cash, that cash is the asset counterpart of the capital market liabilities. If the company buys other assets for that cash, the return on them must be at least as good as its payments commitments to the capital markets. There may appear to be many such opportunities in the boom, but they will almost inevitably bring reduced returns in a recession. If the proceeds of a capital market issue are retained as cash, i.e. banked, then the credit represented by the bank deposits remains the asset counterpart of capital market liabilities. But because it is on the company's account at the bank, it is indistinguishable from internally generated funds, so that it is more likely to be used speculatively on ventures which bring little or no return, or used to service capital market obligations which cannot be 'rolled over' when the capital market is illiquid.[17] In a recession, funds for even prudent fixed capital investment, or the technological improvements necessary to obtain competitive advantage when the recession ends, are much less likely to be forthcoming from the capital markets.

The second principal reason why capital markets are inappropriate sources of finance for fixed capital investment is the uncertainty of returns from productive investment. Conventional theory supposes that, given a certain cost of finance the entrepreneur has merely to compare the expected returns on the available investment projects to be able to decide on those deemed worthwhile, and then issue the appropriate financial liabilities in the markets to finance them. In practice, the actual returns on investment fluctuate according to business cycles and market competition, which cannot be predicted. In a diversified economy a range of industries and firms operate with different degrees of capital intensity. The most capital intensive ones are those that would make the largest calls on the capital market in a boom. These are precisely the industries that are likely to suffer most from excess capacity in a recession, and bear its highest costs.[18]

In such a situation, financing by stock issues means granting an explicit (in the case of bondholders) or implicit (in the case of equity finance) indemnity against loss to the financiers who put up the money, effective as a claim against the assets of the company. In the event of an inability to pay the resulting cash obligations, the company can be ruined. The likelihood of such an eventuality is made greater because capital markets switch between over-capitalizing and under-capitalizing their quoted companies, alongside trade cycles which create fluctuations in companies' sales revenue, and hence oscillations in the value of their productive assets. Such variations are most extreme in the case of capital intensive industries which account for the bulk of fixed capital investment.

It is this fickleness of capital markets that inspired John Maynard Keynes to write his celebrated critique of capital markets:

> Speculators may do no harm as bubbles on a steady stream of enterprise. But the position is serious when enterprise becomes a bubble on a whirlpool of speculation. When the capital development of a country becomes a by-product of the activities of a casino, the job is likely to be ill-done.[19]

However, Keynes was wrong on a matter of empirical fact: it is precisely because of these dangers that established companies try not to finance their fixed capital investment from the capital markets, with the notable exception of investments in buildings where the scarcity of land is thought to place a lower limit on the capital losses that may be sustained by a company. In practice, companies prefer to finance their fixed capital investment out of their reserves (i.e., their accumulated undistributed income) and in Britain some 80 per cent of such investment is financed in this way.[20] An earlier study confirmed that in the United States fixed capital investment is also financed using predominantly internal finance.[21] This is the empirical foundation for the analytical assumption made by post-Keynesians that fixed capital is financed out of corporate sector savings.[22]

If fixed capital investment is financed out of reserves, then the greatest peril that threatens the company is the loss of the reserves that it has committed in this way. Only when its fixed capital investment has 'proven itself' by generating a positive cash flow is a company likely to seek to refinance itself by issuing new capital, in order to top up the liquidity of its reserves, and readjust the structure of the financial liabilities that corresponds to its productive assets. Underlying this is a fundamental principle of corporate finance and the theory of the firm, Kalecki's Principle of Increasing Risk. According to this, the key determinant of a firm's ability to finance investment and growth is the size and liquidity of its reserves. The more external finance is used, the greater are the financial risks of diluting capital ownership, and a company's inability to pay its (financial) capital costs out of its cash flow.[23]

This kind of relationship between industrial and commercial companies and the capital markets has important implications for corporate finance and securities markets. The system whereby capital markets are used to replenish reserves after fixed capital investments have proven themselves suggests a corporate financial structure in which the nominal value of a company's stocks and shares corresponds more or less to the book value of its fixed capital assets. (The difference between the book value of those assets and their historic cost is added to or subtracted from reserves; see Chapter 2.) By aggregation, the book value of the stocks and shares of companies is more or less equal to the book value of the underlying fixed capital assets of those companies.

In a steadily expanding economy, with *rising* investment financed indirectly, in the way described, from capital markets, it is necessary for the cash flow (net of operating costs) of industrial and commercial companies to cover the payments (interest, dividends and net repayments) on those stocks and shares *and* leave a surplus to add to reserves to finance the *growing* fixed capital work in progress. However, because of the trade cycle, this cash flow fluctuates and therefore, to avoid default on their capital market obligations, fixed capital investment expenditures, together with changes in reserves, have to accommodate changes in cash flow. Even companies financing themselves 'prudently' by only re-financing proven fixed capital investments in the capital markets can be over-capitalized as a result of a recession. The degree to which they are embarrassed in this way depends on the ratio of their respective external financing to their own liquid reserves, and the relative fall in sales revenue.

In periods of sanguine optimism, companies may and do issue stock in anticipation of the fruits of their investment. Such financing creates what Minsky calls fragile financial structures, in which capital market liabilities are assumed even before the revenue to pay them is secured.[24] While there is fairly clear empirical evidence that some of this speculative financing happens in practice, this is not a necessary or even central part of the argument here. In this analysis, a capital market issue may be perfectly 'sound' at the time of its sale, in the sense that additional revenue to cover payments on the issue is available from the new productive capacity that is operating normally and being re-financed. It is sufficient for the argument that sales revenue falls as the boom turns into a recession.[25]

The fall in revenue is usually exacerbated by changes in the price of finance which occur over the period of the trade cycle. The yields on stock issues tend to move with (or lag slightly behind) the current rate of interest (with differentials in those yields being determined by the size of the company, its business, and the term of the stock). Interest rates (and hence stock yields) tend to rise as the boom approaches its peak. Companies' interest and dividend obligations therefore tend to rise in a boom *faster* than the rate at which new stock is issued, even if that exactly corresponds to the rate at which fixed capital investments come on stream. In other words, in a boom and even if only re-financing proven investments, companies are increasing their cash flow commitments to capital markets faster than their cash-generating capacity is expanding. This is precisely because in a boom the cash generated by productive fixed capital is rising relative to that capital.

In a recession, the demand for capital market finance tends to dry up, as firms concentrate on maintaining payments on commitments already entered into. Furthermore, the returns from fixed capital investments completed in the recession are now lower than anticipated, providing a less convincing case to the markets for subscribing to new stock that a company may try to issue. Meeting capital market obligations out of diminishing returns from productive assets forces companies to abandon new fixed capital investments. Eventually it may squeeze reserves and oblige companies to lower or even pass their dividends. For this reason, unless a process of capital market inflation is bidding up the prices of stocks, the yield differential between the yield on equities and the yield on bonds tends to reverse itself in a recession: whereas in a boom, the equity yield tends to be less than the yield on bonds (because equities are expected to yield capital gains in addition to their dividends), in a recession the equity yield tends to rise above the bond yield because of the greater likelihood of companies passing their dividends, and shareholders sustaining capital losses on their equity.

Minsky and post-Keynesian theorists argue that over-optimistic expectations make investors and entrepreneurs commit themselves to excessive financial liabilities. In fact, it is the recession of the business cycle that makes otherwise quite realistic expectations over-optimistic. There is a further important difference between this theory and the Financial Instability Hypothesis of Minsky. In the latter, fragile financial structures and instability are created by the change in the composition of capital market liabilities: as the boom proceeds, the ratio of debt to equity is supposed to rise. Minsky's financial crisis is essentially one of over-indebtedness.[26] This may occur in practice but, again, it is not a necessary or central part of our argument. In fact, studies of corporate finance data indicate that, when an economic boom provides them with plentiful sales revenue, firms actually reduce their debt financing, and even replace it with equity (common stock) as the stock market flourishes.[27] However, the Hypothesis may still be valid if equity is regarded like debt as a liability of firms. In effect, equity finance is not a substitute for internal finance because it is a capital market liability rather than a liquid asset. In this analysis, as in Kalecki and Steindl, the key financial ratio is companies' gross gearing (i.e., the ratio of their *total* capital market and bank liabilities to liquid assets), rather than their net gearing (the ratio of debt to liquid assets).[28] Minsky's Financial Instability Hypothesis only stands up to empirical scrutiny if debt and equity are regarded as liabilities of companies, in contrast to the legal fiction that equity is equivalent to entrepreneur's capital.

It is also worth pointing out that the reason why the problem of over-capitalization does not appear in conventional financial theory is that this theory usually presupposes that, for a given company of a particular size and engaged in particular activities, there is an equilibrium set of interest rates according to the term of the obligation. Once obtained, that set of interest rates is supposed to be invariant. In such circumstances, a company issuing stock to replenish its reserves as its fixed capital investments come into production, needs merely to 'invest' the cash raised by its stock issue in financial assets yielding sufficient to cover the dividend and interest payable on the new stock. The company has now entered into the business of intermediation, and the operating profit of the new investment is now available to add to reserves (against the possibility of a downturn in business) or to increase the company's dividend.[29]

However, in practice, a large part of a company's reserves is likely to be tied up in illiquid assets (such as premises or real estate), yielding relatively little cash flow, and capital gains only on sale or realization of the asset. As an insurance against illiquidity in general, another large part of reserves is normally kept in liquid form in bank deposits or on the money markets. The yield on this will decline as interest rates fall, after the onset of the recession. The 'gap' between this yield and the payments due on the capital market obligations issued to fund those reserves will need to be made up from the company's operating profits. In short, it is precisely because, in a recession, the assets of companies deteriorate and are devalued relative to their corresponding capital market liabilities that companies may be said to have been 'over-capitalized' during the preceding boom. Similarly, it is because in a boom those assets improve and increase in value, relative to their corresponding capital market liabilities, that companies may be said to have become 'under-capitalized' during the previous recession.

2 Value and excess in capital markets

Prices are determined in markets by the proportion of the commodities brought to the market for sale to money offered for their purchase.[1]

The view put forward in textbooks of the workings of the capital market is essentially one in which it operates as a market for 'finance' or 'loanable funds'. When considering the price or value of these funds, it is convenient to do it in a *ceteris paribus* way, holding all other factors constant. While this may be a useful way of systematically going through the various circumstances that may affect the value of finance, it advances the fiction that, *given* all these circumstances, the demand for and supply of finance are determined in the capital market by the price of finance. In practice, the supply of finance is determined by income, the institutional arrangements affecting household saving, the financial accumulation of companies and transfers between the capital market and the other vehicles for long-term savings (principally banks and precious metals). In reality, the demand for finance is determined, in the case of companies, by the size and nature of their business and its circumstances, as well as the cost and convenience of alternative financing arrangements. In the case of governments, expenditure commitments and the phase of the business cycle set the balance between government expenditure and revenue, and the government decides as part of its funding policy how that balance is financed between short-term obligations (bills) and bonds.

Thus the demand and supply are not brought into any equilibrium in the capital market. The separate determination of the demand for finance and its supply gives rise to a difference between the finance that is effectively taken out of the market by governments and business, and the actual value of the finance brought into the market and turned over in it. This difference is more than just the distinction commonly made between the primary market (in which capital market issues are sold on behalf of government and business) and the secondary market, the trading between investors of already-issued stocks. The difference between the demand for finance and its supply determines the value turned over in the capital market and, by inflating or deflating it, has a critical effect on the functioning of the market, and the activities of business.

2.1 The value of company securities

To understand how capital markets value securities such as stocks and bonds, it is necessary to distinguish three kinds of valuation. These are notional value or price, actual value or price and effective value or price. The notional value is the value of the company and its securities at the prices advertised by brokers in the market. The actual value of securities is the price at which securities are actually exchanged in the market. Effective value is the price at which they are issued by companies raising funds or refinancing themselves in the market. In order-matching markets, where brokers merely balance the sale and purchase orders which they receive at the price which matches those orders, notional prices are the same as actual prices, or may be the actual prices from the previous trading session. (In this case it is the investors who come to the market with notional, or conditional, prices.) But in the increasingly widespread 'price-driven' markets, in which brokers balance sale and purchase orders by their own purchases and sales and by varying their advertised sale and purchase prices, notional prices will differ from actual prices because not all notional prices will elicit effective offers to buy or sell.

In a modern capitalist economy, in which companies are the vehicles for capital accumulation, the effective value of securities is the important valuation because it affects the actual amount of finance advanced for (refinancing) fixed capital investment by companies. The significance of notional and actual prices is confined to particular capital market transactions that are marginal to the process of fixed capital formation. This is an important consideration in empirical studies of capital markets since notional prices are increasingly used as the basis of capital market valuations of companies. In stock markets where brokers compete for trade by advertising prices, actual prices may deviate quite significantly from notional prices. Yet notional prices can be most conveniently turned into near-continuous price series for the econometric studies. Thus the prices used in empirical studies are frequently not those of actual trade or financing transactions.

However, the total effective market value of all listed securities is merely the total inflow of funds, deducting funds transferred out by investors, into the securities market since the establishment of that market. The indirect capital market financing of fixed capital investment outlined in Chapter 1 means that in theory the total book value (in companies' balance sheets) of companies' securities equals the total book value of their productive assets. If we add in the funds raised by the government, which account for the bulk of actual capital market transactions, we may write the *effective* value at any one time of capital market stocks as the sum of government stocks outstanding at that time and the book value of listed companies' fixed capital:

$$V^e = G + A \qquad\qquad (2.1)$$

where V^e is the book or effective value of stocks in the capital market, G is nominal value of government stocks issued and A is the sum of those companies' net fixed capital investment or bank debt that has been re-financed in the capital markets.

What then determines the *market* or *actual* value of listed company securities? In the case of individual securities, their prices are obviously influenced by circumstances particular to the company and its activities, as well as by the needs of brokers to 'balance their books', i.e., to have sufficient quantities of stocks for trading purposes, but not so much that they can lose money if prices fall.

The actual price of any individual stock may be regarded as the sum of *inflow* and *substitution* effects. Conventional finance theory, perhaps because it is so concerned with portfolio choice, focuses almost entirely on substitution effects. The classic modern investment portfolio theory uses the mean variance of stock prices as indices of risk and to determine 'efficient' portfolios.[2] The so-called 'beta' theory and capital asset pricing models use price movements *relative* to sector, industry or total market *averages* as determinants of risk which then, in circular fashion, are supposed to determine prices relative to industry or total market averages.[3] Arbitrage pricing models use non-financial economic parameters that correlate with returns in excess of a so-called 'risk-free' rate of interest as determinants of market prices.[4] Market efficiency studies focus on the speed of price reversion to market averages and correlations between futures and spot market price changes.[5] These factors may be important when there are zero or negligible net inflows of money into securities markets. However, as net inflows rise, a process of capital market inflation gives an upward trend to prices in general. Moreover, as the amount of buying in the markets is raised by higher inflows, inflows into and outflows out of the markets for particular securities become more extreme. A financial inflow is never translated into equal buying across all markets. Outflows from less favoured markets are therefore enhanced by investors' portfolio switches to take advantage of capital gains in markets favoured by inflows. In such a situation, substitution effects between the prices of particular stocks become unstable and unpredictable. This is further discussed in Chapters 6 and 10.

The net inflow into securities markets may be notionally divided into two parts. One part is equal to the total book value of listed companies' productive assets, which is of course the sum of those companies' net fixed capital investment and bank debt that has been re-financed in the capital markets, plus the funds raised by the government. In an industrial economy (as was noted above) the re-investment of profits is the mainspring of capital accumulation by companies. The total book value of their capital stock, less bank debt re-financing, represents their total accumulation of profits. The other part is the net inflow of funds into the companies' securities market that is *in excess* of that re-financing. It is this excess net inflow that inflates the *actual* value of securities above, or deflates them below, the book value of listed companies' productive assets and the nominal debt issue of the government.[6]

In any one period, therefore, the market or actual value of securities, V^a, is equal to the effective value of those securities plus the excess net inflow times the number of times that it is turned over in the capital market (its velocity of circulation – see below), i.e., the total of government stocks outstanding, the total profits of quoted companies accumulated as productive capital, A, *plus* the accumulated excess net inflow of funds into the capital market, I, times its average velocity of circulation, V:

$$V^a = V^e + v.I = G + A + v.I \tag{2.2}$$

In any given *period*, therefore, the *change* in the actual value of securities, $V^{a'}$, may be divided into the change in the government stocks outstanding, G', plus the change in the companies' productive stock refinanced in the capital market, A', and the additional excess net inflow of funds into the capital market during that period times its velocity of circulation, $v.I'$, i.e.:

$$V^{a'} = V^{e'} + v.I' = G' + A' + v.I' \tag{2.3}$$

In an economy where the personal and overseas sectors are balanced, the net financial inflow into businesses from their trading activities or their gross profits is, by definition, more or less equal to investment.[7] For the term A', the net addition to the productive capacity of companies in the period, the gross profits earned by those businesses during that period may then be substituted. This shows the change in the market value of listed company securities *as it appears to participants in the capital market*, namely as the sum of the profits accruing to listed companies, and the net excess inflow of funds into the capital market during that period.[8]

The net excess inflow is, in turn, a function of changes in profits, the recent trend in securities prices (see Chapter 1, section 1.1 above), institutional factors (such as changes in welfare state provision, which affect personal saving behaviour, and changes in the demographic structure of the population, which affect the balance of personal financial accumulation, as opposed to consumption out of savings – see Part II), and changes in the rate of interest, which affect investors' preferences between the company securities, government bonds, bank deposits and other forms of wealth in their portfolios of accumulated savings.[9]

Changes in profits and trends in stock prices attract savings from other non-financial securities markets, such as bank deposits, gold and property, which also act as repositories for savings. Profits are perceived as an important determinant of the inflow of funds into capital markets because higher profits mean higher earnings per share, higher dividend cover, an enhanced ability to service company debt and the prospect of increased dividends. However, this is just how the matter appears to agents in the capital markets:

the vital element underlying profits is the fixed capital investment which creates the capacity to generate the cash flows of listed companies and transforms savings into sales revenue.

The excess net inflow (I') may be positive or negative in any one period of time, as is clearly indicated in the previous chapter's analysis of the over-capitalization and under-capitalization of companies. What happens if there is a negative excess net inflow of funds, i.e., if the net inflow of funds into the capital markets is less than the amounts of fixed capital investment that companies are seeking to re-finance? According to conventional theory, prices fall and the rise in bond and dividend yields is supposed to stimulate the inflow of funds into the capital market and discourage the issuing of new securities by companies unwilling to pay higher dividends or interest.

In this context, Tobin's 'q' theory may be interpreted as arguing that net excess inflows are balanced by companies' net investments or disinvestment in their fixed capital assets. This has the merit of recognizing that stock market conjunctures affect the amount of capital market liabilities that firms are prepared to assume. But it is wrong as a theory of investment.[10] In reality, as stock prices fall, the flow of funds into the capital markets is actually discouraged, and brokers and issuing houses have difficulty in selling new stock. Companies cannot re-finance completed capital investments, i.e., the corporate sector cannot sell part or all of the new securities that it wishes to sell to replenish the reserves that have been tied up in productive investment. This squeeze on company liquidity discourages further fixed capital investment. Other companies seeking to 'roll over' maturing debt or loan stocks may find themselves unable to do so, so that their liquidity is squeezed as they repay maturing debts.

The degree to which company liquidity is drained by their inability to roll over debt depends on the amount of outstanding debt that is due to mature in this period. Let us suppose that companies have sensibly protected themselves against such an eventuality, according to conventional wisdom, by financing themselves only with equity. If the net excess outflow still exceeds the amount that companies wish to re-finance (i.e., the financial sector is a net seller of stocks), the stock market will crash until financial investors or rentiers are persuaded to stop selling and/or start buying stock again. Thus equity financing may cause the market to crash precisely because there is not a stock of maturing debt or loan stocks to induce the company sector to buy in rentiers' excess desired stock sales.

When the excess net inflow of funds is positive, there are more than enough funds in the market to re-finance companies' fixed capital projects, and government debt issues. The excess is then taken up by a higher turnover of the available stocks and higher stock prices, as brokers and investors are obliged to offer higher prices in order to persuade holders of stocks to sell. Again, conventional theory supposes that the high price of stocks will discourage the inflow of funds into the capital market, and encourage firms to undertake more investment. In reality, however, *rising* prices encourage still higher inflows of funds into the market. Unless companies supply additional stocks into the market, rentiers' excess demand will continue to force prices up until that excess demand is eliminated by a change of expectations or the inflow is re-directed to other markets. Furthermore, as noted in the previous chapter, conditions in the capital market have little or no influence on the amount of fixed capital investment that companies undertake (because of the Principle of Increasing Risk). High stock prices merely encourage companies to re-finance *in excess of their current needs*. This is another factor giving rise to the over-capitalization which is described above.

Thus, in a process of capital market inflation, where there is over a longer period a positive excess net cash inflow into the financial markets, first notional prices and then actual prices are driven up until effective prices reach a level that elicits the issue of sufficient new stock to take up the positive net inflow, or until the positive inflow ceases. An excess net inflow circulates in the capital market raising prices in this way until it is fully intermediated, i.e., when it is taken out of the market. Unlike a portfolio 'switch' in which the increased demand for a stock (or stocks) is cancelled out by the additional supply of other stock, an excess net inflow gets passed around the market successively, appearing as additional demand for more and more stocks. The successive increments in demand for stocks multiplies the initial excess inflow into the markets.

This multiplier is a kind of velocity of circulation of money in the capital market, except that it is not a stable variable because there is no fixed or balancing relationship between the money coming into the market, actual, notional or effective prices, and the amount of stock being sold. An excess inflow from a particular period rapidly taken out by a change in investors' liquidity preference may have minimal effect on stock prices. That same excess inflow, left to circulate for longer in the market, may cause prices to rise considerably before it is taken out of the market. Arbitrage opportunities, arising out of differences between notional and actual prices, cause the inflow to circulate more rapidly. This velocity of circulation is also affected by financial and institutional innovation. Computerization, advances in telecommunications and deregulation have greatly abbreviated the procedures involved in buying and selling stock. These changes have increased the velocity of circulation of money in the capital markets, so that a given inflow of money in a given period results in an even greater increase in actual prices.

These considerations may be summarized and illustrated by extending equation 2.3 to incorporate the flow of funds in the economy at large. This flow of funds is conventionally summed up in the saving identity, obtained by subtracting consumption from the equation between income and expenditure. According to this identity, the total saving in the economy over a given period of time, S, is by definition equal to the gross investment expenditure in the economy, E_i, plus the fiscal deficit (government expenditure, E_g, minus fiscal revenue, T), plus the trade surplus (exports, X, minus imports, M):

$$S = E_i + (E_g - T) + (X - M)$$

In a system in which saving is intermediated through banks and securities markets, deducting from this identity the flow of savings into the banking system, S_b, gives the flow of savings into the capital or securities market. The latter is then equal to the change in outstanding government securities, G', plus the change in outstanding corporate securities, A', plus the excess net inflow of funds into the securities market, I':

$$G' + A' + I' = E_i + (E_g - T) + (X - M) - S_b \tag{2.4}$$

(For the sake of simplicity here, as earlier, it is assumed that there are no international portfolio capital flows: corporate securities are issued by domestically registered companies, government securities are issued by the government in whose jurisdiction the market is found, and investors, or rentiers, invest at home. This assumption could be removed without changing the analysis in its essentials. But the addition to the scope of the analysis would be trivial by comparison with the increased complications to the present discussion.)

Re-arranging equation 2.4 gives an equation for the net excess inflow into the capital market:

$$I' = [E_i - A' + (X - M)] + [(E_g - T) - G'] - S_b \tag{2.5}$$

The first term in squared brackets on the right-hand side of the equation represents the financial balance of companies' investment activity plus their profits from trading abroad: $E_i - A'$ is companies' gross investment expenditure minus their net new issue of bonds. As has been argued, investment expenditure is overwhelmingly financed from liquid reserves, equivalent to bank deposits. $E_i - A'$ therefore is the corporate sector's net investment expenditure funded by drawing down bank deposits or bank borrowing.

The second term in squared brackets on the right-hand side of the equation is the balance between the government's fiscal deficit $(E_g - T)$ and its net bond issue (G'). In other words, it represents the government's net bank-financed expenditure.

The final term, $- S_b$, represents the net outflow of saving from the bank sector. This is an indicator of what Keynes called the speculative demand for money, which can be more broadly called investors' or rentiers' liquidity preference.

The net excess of inflow of funds into the capital market in a given period is therefore equal to:

> companies' profits from trading overseas *plus* their bank-financed investment, *plus*
> the government's net bank-financed expenditure, *minus*
> the net addition to bank savings.

It should be borne in mind that equation 2.5 is derived from definitional identities for the actual value of the stock market and saving in the economy. No causal inference may be made directly from it. But it is possible to identify those elements in the equation which are subject to individual, firms' or government discretion. The securities market as a whole cannot decide to receive a net excess inflow. But companies can decide how much to invest, and how to pay for that investment (even if the corporate sector as a whole cannot determine the current account balance of payments). Similarly, the government can decide how to finance its deficit, even if that deficit may be as much under the influence of general business and economic conditions as it is under the control of fiscal policy makers. Finally, barring the occasional illiquidity of the stock market, savers themselves, or their agents, decide how to allocate their savings between that market and the banking system.

If equation 2.5 is then multiplied through by v, the number of times this excess net inflow is turned over in the capital market, and then added to the net bond issue of the government (G′) and the net securities issue of the sector (A′), the result is an extended equation for the actual value of the securites market in the period, i.e.:

$$V^{a'} = G' + A' + v.E_i + v.(E_g - T) + v.(X - M) - vS_b$$

re-arranging gives:

$$V^{a'} = G'(1-v) + A'(1-v) + v[E_i + (E_g - T) + (X - M) - S_b] \qquad (2.6)$$

The term in square brackets on the right-hand side is obviously the saving identity, minus the addition to bank saving. The analysis can be further simplified by assuming that there are only capitalists, earning profits, and workers (including government employees) earning wages in the economy. The saving identity therefore represents workers' saving, S_w, plus capitalists' saving. If workers' saving is deducted from the saving identity, the remaining saving is that of the capitalists. If capitalists' consumption, C_c, is added to their saving the result is the balance of capitalists' income and expenditure, i.e. profits equalling capitalists' comsumption and their saving. In this way the saving identity can be extended to give Kalecki's equation for profits (R):

$$R = E_i + (E_g - T) + (X - M) + C_c - S_w$$

Since $R = S + C_c - S_w$, this profits equation, minus capitalists' consumption plus workers' saving may be substituted for the saving identity in equation 2.6. This gives:

$$V^{a'} = (G' + A')(1-v) + v(R - C_c + S_w - S_b) \qquad (2.7)$$

Equation 2.7 gives a relationship between the values of the stock market in a given period and total, rather than individual, profits in the economy. The stock market is positively affected by profits and workers' saving (the latter is discussed in Part II), but it is negatively influenced by capitalists' consumption and bank-mediated saving.

Overall, the equation shows the actual value of the stock market to be a complex balance of the financial flows in the economy that are intermediated through the capital market. Since one would expect the money put into the market to be turned over more than once before it is taken out by the government or the corporate sector, v in any extended period, such as a year, is likely to be greater than one. The term (1-v) in the first part of the equation's right-hand side is therefore a negative factor representing the effect on the value of stock market turnover of increasing the stock issues of government and the company sector. The second part of the equation represents the positive effect on stock market turnover of profits and workers' saving, but diminished by capitalists' consumption and liquidity preference expressed as saving inflows into the banking system.

An excess inflow may be taken out by an investor taking money out of the market after selling his stocks. In this case, the excess net inflow is eliminated (liquidated perhaps?). It may be taken out by the government issuing bonds. However, this will be determined by its fiscal and monetary policy, rather than by the state of liquidity in the capital market (see Chapter 2, section 2.2). Finally, it may be taken out by listed companies issuing stocks in excess of those needed to refinance their investments. In this way, the apparent liquidity and high activity of inflated markets, which observers mistake for signs of perfect competition, is simply an excess net inflow of funds looking for someone to take it out of the market.

Why should companies wish to issue more stocks than they need to re-finance their investments? They may wish to replace bank debt with cheaper stock issues. But if the excess net inflow is sufficiently great to inflate the capital markets, then there is an additional incentive to issue stock to finance mergers, takeovers, deglomerations and various other kinds of corporate restructurings. These enable companies in effect to become corporate rentiers making a profit on the sale and purchase of companies as capital market inflation raises the value of assets which can be sold in that market. This is further discussed in Chapters 3 and 6.

Capital market inflation has important consequences for the structure of the capital market. Such inflation enhances with capital gains the return to investors on long-term stocks. Such capital gains are proportionate to the term of the stock, which sets the date by which its value must revert to its redemption price. At one extreme, the shortest term securities, company or Treasury bills due to mature in the following day or two show virtually no capital gain if the capital market is inflated, because they will be shortly re-paid at face value, and only at face value. At the other extreme, the longest term securities, namely shares or common stock, show the largest gains due to capital market inflation, because there is no maturity value to limit the increase in their actual price. Therefore capital market inflation increases investors' or rentiers' preference for longer-term stocks in general, and their appetite for shares or common stock in particular.

Such a shift in investors' preferences obviously offers companies the possibility of increased financing with the more long-term stocks, the interest cost of which can be fixed at the lowest rate by issuing or rolling over stock at a time when stock yields are low. The best financing of all, in this situation, is equity or common stock issue, securing funds which never have to be repaid at an annual dividend cost which the company in theory may set in accordance with its current financial situation.

Capital market inflation is supposed to reduce the yield on stock: for a given dividend or coupon (interest rate) a higher price is supposed to mean a lower yield. In fact the reduction in this market yield is offset by the additional return of capital gain which such inflation introduces into the capital market. This inflation lengthens the average term of stocks at the cost of a structural weakening of the capital market in two respects: investors or rentiers become more dependent on demand from other investors to secure the liquidity and capital gains on their longer-term investments, and companies increase the proportion of their financing which is non-refundable and on which they may make what are in theory discretionary annual payments. However, it takes a slackening of capital market inflation for this structural weakness to become apparent. Such inflation therefore generates Ponzi finance. This is further investigated in Part II of this book.

In a process of capital market deflation or disintermediation, actual prices fall until rentiers (or investors) are discouraged from selling stock, or effective prices reach such a level that elicits sufficient repurchases or redemptions of stock by companies to provide an inflow of funds from the corporate sector that balances the outflow required by investors or rentiers. In markets where traders and investors place orders in response to price changes (as opposed to the order-matching system that prevails in many continental European markets) actual prices normally change from hour to hour. However, the mere possibility that actual prices may drive effective prices to levels which match financial inflows (purchases of stock) into the capital market from the company sector to financial outflows desired by rentiers or investors does not mean that the market is ever in equilibrium. The balance between desired sales and purchases in the market is in practice made up by changes in the inventories of stocks held by brokers and frustrated or induced capital market transactions of rentiers and companies.

In a capital market inflation, takeover (mergers and acquisitions) and capital restructuring sentiment in the corporate sector may motivate an additional issue of stock. But in a capital market deflation it is much more difficult to persuade companies to buy in stock, even if actual stock values fall below effective (issue) values thereby making it profitable for companies to redeem stock at lower prices than those at which they were issued. In the first place, the corporate sector historically has drawn funds from the capital markets, in order to re-finance illiquid productive capital assets, rather than supplying them to the markets. The ability of companies to buy in stock is circumscribed by their liquidity. Hence, when investors on balance seek to take funds out of the market (in the terminology used above, the excess net outflow is negative), the capital market crashes, i.e., it ceases to be able to transact sale orders. While crashes may be avoided by having highly capitalized brokers with the liquidity to buy in the excess sales of rentiers, the brokers' capacity to buy in such net sales depends on the amount of their liquidity relative to those excess sales.[11] Rentiers' net excess sales in turn depend in part on how much they purchased in the first place. An extended period of capital market inflation is therefore more likely to give rise to larger desired outflows by rentiers. Maintaining the liquidity of longer-term stocks (see above and Chapter 6) therefore requires brokers' liquidity to rise in proportion to the inflation of the market.

The excess net inflow into the capital market therefore constitutes a margin of safety for the market. When a disintermediation occurs because financial investors wish on balance to sell stock, the market is kept stable not by having prices change rapidly to induce less selling and more buying but by the accumulation of past net excess inflows out of which brokers can purchase the excess stocks that investors now wish to sell. Thus stock markets crash not because they are out of equilibrium, but because their disequilibrium has been insufficient.

It is useful to consider here briefly why these changes in the structure of the capital market, with its inflation and deflation, have not been noted by orthodox finance theorists. Orthodox finance theory, from Walras, through Miller and Modigliani, to McKinnon and Shaw and 'efficient market' theories, are based on optimizing equilibrium. This is a utopian and teleological approach in which theorists put forward a view of the markets that does not start from how they have emerged and how they actually operate, but from an imagined universe in which the problems of liquidity and ephemeral markets are systematically eliminated. Explicitly, or by implication, they suggest that measures of deregulation and capital market inflation bring the real world closer to this perfectly competetive financial utopia.

Orthodox theory arrives at this presumed equilibrium by having the financing and liquidity preferences of companies determined in the capital markets. From taking those exogenous factors which determine the financing requirements of business as *given*, for analytical purposes, it moves illicitly to the notion that these requirements are set by the prices in the markets for finance. In this way, orthodox finance theory makes financing requirements equal to the supply of funds at a given price, so that trade in capital markets only occurs when the net excess inflow of funds is zero. There is therefore no change in the structure of the capital market. An alternative equilibrating mechanism may be through the liquidity preference of investors, with any excess net inflow accommodated by an appropriate change in the liquidity preference of investors. But when a positive excess net inflow raises the price of longer-term stocks (and by implication also reduces their market yield) it also offers holders of the stock the possibility of capital gain if the positive excess net inflow is sustained. This prospective capital gain offsets the fall in market yield, reducing the incentive of investors to switch to more short-term, liquid stocks. Equilibrating changes in liquidity preference are correspondingly weaker in periods of capital market inflation. However, in its determination to see equilibrium as the only final outcome of markets, the orthodox theory only takes note of 'equilibrating mechanisms', and regulations which distort these mechanisms. With equilibrium, financial innovation and the increasing activity in the longer-term stocks may be portrayed triumphantly as advances in the scope of market relations and in the finance which is supposed to be available for productive employment.

In the second place, it is convenient for orthodox finance theory to assume universal arbitrage. This is so that supply and demand functions for particular types of finance, in which given quantities of finance are supplied and demanded at unique prices in individual markets, will converge to an equilibrium price and quantity of funds supplied and demanded. Here too the presumption is that financing requirements, and the supply of investible funds, are determined by the prices in the capital market. To obtain a unique price for each amount of finance supplied or demanded, it is necessary to exclude all other prices by assuming that arbitrage would eliminate them. Universal arbitrage means that demand for stocks is price-elastic: sellers need merely to reduce their price marginally in order to be flooded with orders to buy their stocks. In this situation, the liquidity of the market is always perfect, or is potentially so.

The net excess inflow does not just affect the liquidity of the capital market. It also influences the relative prices of different classes of financial instruments. In general, changes in bond prices are mutually determined by the interest rates on various classes and maturities of financial assets, but they have a fixed maturity value. Accordingly, equity prices, with prospects of greater capital gain, and their turnover, respond disproportionately to inflows into capital markets or company profits and excess net inflows. Thus, in a boom, equity prices rise faster than bond prices. In a recession, they fall more rapidly than bond prices. This is yet another reason why the difference between the yield on equities and bond yield becomes negative in a boom and positive in a recession. Portfolio managers also switch to equities in a boom to secure capital gains, and switch to bonds in a recession to avoid capital losses. These changes in demand further enhance this yield differential.

As the mix of demand for equity and bonds changes over the cycle, so too does the mix of financing that is financially most advantageous for companies: equity (common stock) affords them cheaper funds than bonds in a boom, and the situation is reversed in a recession. Yet the optimum combination of debt and equity for a company depends on the nature of its business, principally the amount of capital equipment that it uses and its profit cycle. The switching of the yield gap may therefore encourage companies to deviate from their optimum gearing. This is another disturbance, albeit a minor one compared with the more general disequilibrium described above, that may be transmitted from capital markets to companies, and through them to the economy as a whole.

In summary then, actual prices are largely determined by the net excess inflow into (or outflow from) the capital market, and the length of time during which that net excess inflow stays in the market before it is taken out, or intended sales of securities are balanced by purchases. The movement of actual prices as capital market inflation proceeds is distinct from the movement of notional prices.

In modern capital markets trading is accompanied by a permanent buzz of new 'information'. Notional prices are principally influenced by news or 'statsbabble', the process by which economic and financial statistics, shorn of their methodological limitations, are propelled around the market by traders using them to arouse speculative intents and desires among investors or rentiers. ('Statsbabble' is further discussed in Chapter 7, note 16.) Such notional prices are thus the true, but limited, domain of theories of 'efficient' markets, which see financial markets as information-processing systems, rather than as financial intermediaries.

Whereas actual prices are discrete, notional prices are continuous, which makes them suitable for stock derivatives and aggregating into the continuous-time stock indices that are the basis of stock index derivatives. When frequent trades occur, notional prices may be made up of a string of actual prices. But when trade is less frequent they may, and often do, diverge. A small net inflow of funds, coupled with falling notional prices due to 'bearish' news, may cause that inflow to circulate that much more rapidly as investors more readily find bargains for their money. But this situation will also discourage sales of stock at lower prices to take out the inflow. A net outflow combined with rising notional prices will leave actual prices trailing behind notional prices.

Finally, effective prices are not in practice the terms on which companies undertake productive investment, as implied by the textbook notion that the risk-adjusted yield on securities is the cost of financing and the opportunity cost of that investment. Whereas actual prices are principally determined by the net inflow into the capital market, and notional prices are principally determined by a conventional interpretation of news and statistics, effective prices are influenced on the demand side by the adjustments that companies make through the capital market to their balance sheets and their liquidity.

2.2 Some policy issues

The foregoing analysis describes a very specific relationship between capital markets and companies. It seems to summarize fairly well the circumstances in those economies with autonomous stock markets, such as the US and the

UK.[12] The extent to which it is a general theory depends on whether it applies as well to other capitalist economies, in particular those with a universal banking tradition such as in France, Germany and Italy, in which large banks subsume the functions of a capital market and countries entering the capitalist path of economic development.

In continental Europe, entrepreneurs and bankers influenced by the ideas of the French social philosopher Saint-Simon developed general banking as the form of the capital market.[13] Typically, the banks lend to companies and re-finance that lending at a later date by converting it into equity, which is then sold to the banks' customers, or taken into the banks' own portfolio.

Such a system allows a company to increase its ratio of debt to reserves with greater security, because of the greater ease of conversion of debt into shareholders' equity. A consequence of this arrangement is that, over an extended period, it becomes a system of bank capitalism, in which banks hold effectively controlling interests in the largest industrial corporations. The Principle of Increasing Risk still applies, especially among smaller companies and businesses which are not in a position to elicit accommodating credit from their bank shareholder more or less on demand. The amount of secure lending to a company, given the business in which it is engaged, still depends on the amount of its accumulated reserves. Such lending is now more likely to finance fixed capital investment in anticipation of the returns from that investment when it is completed. But this is simply another way of saying that a certain quantum of reserves can finance a larger amount of fixed capital investment at the cost of bringing forward capital market (banks') claims against the company. The disadvantage of earlier external financing claims is offset by the greater liquidity (access to credit) that general banking offers to its corporate clients.

Equity holdings by banks are generally recognized as reducing under-capitalization in a recession, when short-term borrowing is more easily converted into longer-term capital market liabilities. This may ease any difficulties in turning over short-term borrowing. However, whether this also reduces over-capitalization (an excessive rise in the *gross* gearing ratio) depends on the ease with which those liabilities can be effectively reduced (in the sense of diminishing claims on the current cash flow of companies) in a recession. Merely changing the composition of outstanding liabilities between bank debt, bonds and equity (common stocks), which are increasingly similar liabilities (see above), may not necessarily do this.

The general banking system therefore alters the particulars, but not the fundamental elements, of this analysis of the relationship between capital markets and companies. However, in such a system securities are rarely traded and are usually purchased for income, rather than rapid gain. Financial fragility may still arise, as it does in all banking systems in a market economy. But general banking is less prone to capital market inflation, because bankers have not discovered how to make companies take out loans

as effectively as a booming capital market can persuade companies to partic-
ipate in corporate financial restructurings.

In practice, these differences between capitalist economies with general
banking systems and those with active capital markets are decreasing.
Governments in virtually all capitalist countries have taken measures to
promote more active capital markets, wider share ownership and pensions
schemes funded in capital markets. In France, tax concessions have been
given to encourage personal saving in stock market investment funds. Insofar
as this entails the transfer of savings from general banks it will, in accordance
with the above analysis, mean a corresponding transfer of corporate liabilities from more flexible general banking liabilities, to less flexible capital
market liabilities. This, in turn, will destabilize company liquidity, although
this may not be obvious in the first flush of inflating markets. Insofar as the
move towards more active capital markets increases the actual amount of
funds invested in company securities, the corresponding increase in company
liabilities is likely to increase company holdings of liquid assets (to reduce the
risk of illiquidity), rather than fixed capital investment, as intended by
proponents of capital markets.[14]

This analysis also has important and critical implications for the financing
of small businesses and companies in developing countries. Both are widely
recognized as having their expansion excessively constrained by a shortage of
finance for (fixed capital) investment. However, the central financial problem
of small companies is not their lack of external financing opportunities, as is
commonly thought. Rather, it is their lack of accumulated reserves or
sources of internal finance. A prudent gearing ratio for a small business
warrants a smaller amount of external finance than could be serviced by a
larger company with larger reserves.

Much the same is true of companies in the informal sector of developing
countries and indigenous companies in general in less-developed economies,
where the World Bank and the International Monetary Fund have been
urging the establishment of capital markets.[15] The view of these institutions
is in line with the current orthodoxy on financial development in the work of
McKinnon and Shaw. According to them, undeveloped finance and financial
regulation amount to 'financial repression', where indiscriminate 'distortions
of financial prices including interest rates and foreign exchange rates' holds
down 'the real rate of (economic) growth and the real size of the financial
system, relative to non-financial magnitudes. In all cases this strategy has
stopped or gravely retarded the development process.'[16] The McKinnon-
Shaw view now provides the chief intellectual justification for the capital
market inflation in developing countries, which is discussed further in
Chapter 5.

The shortage of internal financial resources in small and developing
companies is, of course, made more acute by the fact that capital equipment
is not easily divisible, especially in primary and manufacturing industries.
There, the amount of equipment required just to get started may be very

large by comparison with the internal funds available to the entrepreneur.[17] Medium and larger companies, concentrated in the developed capitalist countries, have larger liquid reserves with which to finance their fixed capital investments. In practice they also use the capital markets as suggested here to re-finance those investments on completion. An excess of external finance may account for the higher failure rate of small businesses and indigenous enterprises in developing countries.[18]

There is a third set of policy implications for takeover (merger and acquisition) activity, which is widely regarded as the cutting edge of the capital market's influence over quoted companies. It is common nowadays to regard the capital markets as markets in company ownership, driven by takeover booms that force slothful company managers to 'make their assets work'.[19] Takeovers in fact enhance the inclination towards the over-capitalization of companies during an economic boom, motivated by the same volatile expectations that move the capital markets.[20] Where financed with cash, such bids transfer corporate liquidity out of the bidding company and into the capital market. Where market liquidity is stable and assured, this may not adversely affect companies' liquidity. But where market liquidity is volatile, this may leave companies which have depleted their cash reserves on acquisitions unable to re-finance their balance sheets later on.

In view of this and the general tendency towards over-capitalization and under-capitalization even when takeovers are strictly controlled, it is worth considering how the adverse effects of capital markets on corporate liquidity may be alleviated. One simple solution (short of entirely reforming the capital markets, together with the system of corporate finance) would be to force interest rates steadily down as a boom proceeds, so that companies' capital market commitments do not rise faster than their cash flow-generating capacity.[21] However, this would be contrary to all known principles of sound finance and monetary policy, including orthodox Keynesianism (in contrast to Keynes) and monetarism. Reducing interest rates is usually regarded as invoking a looser monetary policy that may increase inflation in a boom when prices in the economy at large are already likely to be increasing. It may also encourage even more excessive re-financing by companies during the boom. To be effective the manoeuvre would have to alter the composition of capital market liabilities in such a way as to reduce the aggregate claim of those liabilities on company cash flow in anticipation of the following recession. This is more easily done by the switch to equity (common stock) financing which occurs as capital market inflation proceeds, and which finances companies at the cost of the stability of the capital markets. (This point is further explained below.) In the case of bonds, a lower rate of interest would only reduce payments on new bonds or floating rate bonds.

Ultimately, the manipulation of interest rates and the 'fixing' of prices in capital markets as a means of stabilizing investment misses the whole point of the Principle of Increasing Risk, namely that the growth in a company's own resources relative to its capital market liabilities is a better influence on fixed capital investment.[22] The resources that a company can obtain in the capital market have liabilities against them that are potentially ruinous in a recession. The resources that a company obtains through trade entail no such liabilities. Governments that wish to encourage fixed capital investment at home and economic development abroad should buy from companies and poorer countries in order to provide them with investible funds that do not carry with them financial risks.

A second way of regulating the capital market is by open market operations. This method would require the government to vary its bond issue in accordance with the inflow of funds in the capital market, relative to companies' re-financing needs. The government would then issue bonds to take out of the market any excess net inflow, and then buy bonds in to reverse any net capital outflow by rentiers.

An obvious problem with this kind of regulation would be that it may be incompatible with the central bank's more traditional open market operations to take out excess liquidity from the banking system. Because the capital market cannot be separated financially from the banking system, 'round-tripping' may occur if the government is selling in one market and buying in the other. In 'round-tripping' traders would exploit price differences of similar bonds in the two markets. Such price anomalies would attract further inflows, rather than diminish them.

More critically, open market operations could seriously destabilize government finances and monetary policy over the business cycle. Typically, in a boom, the government has a financial surplus, or a modest deficit. A more serious deficit arises in a recession, when more bonds are liable to be issued. However, the excess net cash inflow into the capital market in a boom is usually large, with net excess outflows or redemptions starting as the boom ends and the recession takes hold. Open market operations to stabilize the capital market would therefore require enhanced government bond issues in a boom and bond purchasing in a recession. With the government's financing requirements being exactly the reverse of this, the government would end up having to issue money or bills in the recession not only to cover its own financial deficit, but also to finance its bond purchases. In a boom, an enhanced bond issue would eliminate the need for the issue of bills. The resulting shortage of liquidity in the banking system may be a useful discipline on speculative advances by banks, but excess liquidity in the banking system in a recession could seriously destabilize that system.[23]

Another partial solution to the over-capitalization problem would be a system of capital market finance through equity, discouraging the issue of bonds. This would allow capital market finance to be raised at low yields in a boom and reduce the problems for companies of rolling over debt in a recession, when capital market liquidity, unless inflated, is low. In the recession, companies could be encouraged to reduce their dividends to conserve their internal liquidity. However, this may not be appropriate to the financing needs of the particular line of business in which a company is involved (see above). It would require companies to dilute ownership as they grow, and may cause investors seeking fixed returns to abandon the corporate securities market in favour of government debt.

Furthermore, as was noted above, equity is still a capital market liability and the cash raised by it is not the same as internal funds, but remains the asset counterpart of that liability. A company financed entirely by equity issues may still find itself excessively geared, if its capital market value exceeds the actual value of its productive assets. Keynes mentions in his *General Theory* considering the possibility of making 'the purchase of an investment permanent and indissoluble, like marriage, except by reason of death or other grave cause'. In his view, 'this would force the investor to direct his mind to the long-term prospects and to those only'. He concluded that it would also reduce the supply of risk capital.[24]

But equity (or common stock) finance destabilizes the capital market, removing the possibility, when there is a net outflow of funds from the market, of drawing funds from the corporate sector as companies' debts and loans mature. Bond finance may stabilize capital markets, but this is at the expense of higher servicing costs for companies when interest rates are high in a boom, and at the risk of not being able to roll over debt in a recession. Compared with debt, equity finance provides greater financial benefits for companies at the cost of a greater risk of illiquidity in the capital market.

Capital markets therefore work with limited efficiency in re-financing companies and allowing stockholders to adjust their portfolios. Capital markets are not the central capital-allocating mechanism of a capitalist economy, as has been suggested by virtually all economists since Walras. Unstable capital inflows and the trade cycle tend to destabilize capital markets, and this volatility in turn disturbs the efficiency with which capital markets can provide liquidity for companies. Therefore, insofar as capital markets play an active part in fixed capital investment decisions and the financing of such investments, such instability will tend also to disturb fixed capital investment and exacerbate the trade cycle. Capital market inflation has adverse consequences for listed companies and the economy as a whole because the resulting excessive gearing discourages investment and eventually drains the internal liquidity of companies that is not held against financial market liabilities. Internal corporate liquidity, rather than the liquidity of capital markets, is crucial for fixed capital investment. Capital market inflation also has adverse consequences for investors and the structure of capital markets. It adds to the return on stocks an element of capital gain which can only be secured by continued inflation. In this way, it creates in the capital market unstable Ponzi financing structures. These are further discussed in the next chapter.

Part II
Ponzi finance and pension fund capitalism

3 Pension funds and Ponzi finance

In Part I of this book, the relationship between capital markets and companies was examined. Mention was made there of the possibility that a regime of growing excess financial inflows into capital markets, or capital market inflation, may create an apparent abundance of liquidity and rising values in the markets, which would not be applied to companies' real investment in fixed capital. Part II of this book discusses funded pension schemes. These are the main impetus behind the inflation of capital markets in the main industrialized countries since the 1970s. Some of the consequences of the resulting extended capital market inflation for privatization and monetary policy are considered. It is argued that funded pension schemes make the economy less efficient and weaken the financial system. They do this by putting large irregular flows of contractual savings into capital markets, needing an ever-expanding contributing labour force to sustain those flows and prices in securities markets. Contribution inflows are limited by the fall in rates of inflation in the advanced capitalist countries, the size of the well-paid labour force and by the trend towards the casualization of labour, which makes pension fund saving a less appropriate form of saving. The reduced financial inflows into pension funds will reduce the liquidity of capital markets and thwart the eventual disintermediation from securities markets.

3.1 Pension funds, banking and industrial investment

The virtues of funded pension schemes have come to be a part of the core orthodoxy of finance and finance theory in the 1990s. Few economic doctrines have become as incontrovertible as the wisdom of relieving taxpayers of the burden of paying for retirement pensions, and channelling pension fund contributions into securities markets to provide savings for the finance of capital investment. Governments in the US and the UK pride themselves on their low commitment to support their ageing populations, while governments in Continental Europe, facing the self-imposed fiscal austerity required for European Economic and Monetary Union, are embarrassed by the supposed generosity of their state pension provision. As a corollary to this, capital markets in the US and the UK luxuriate in huge inflows of pension contributions, while Continental Europe's capital markets worry about their governments' growing indebtedness.

Part II of this book is not concerned with whether indeed there is an 'ageing' problem, or whether state pensions are better than funded pension schemes. This has already been the subject of exhaustive study.[1] Rather, Part II critically analyses the financial and economic consequences of funding pension liabilities in order to understand better that peculiar combination of financial market inflation and instability with economic stagnation that seems to characterize capitalist economies at the turn of the century.

The introduction of funded pension schemes gives rise to a huge inflow of contributions, which are used to buy securities, i.e., stocks and shares, and company and government bills. This is especially so when the schemes are very 'immature', i.e., at the beginning of the life of a funded scheme, when contributions are coming in, but those retiring have not been in the schemes long enough to 'buy' any more than very small pensions entitlements from them. In this way, and on a sufficient scale, the contributions inflow (net of pensions payments) ends up inflating securities markets. When funded pension schemes were being advocated during the 1970s, one of their supposed main advantages was that they would provide long-term finance for business expansion. In practice, as explained below, the situation is rather more complicated than this.

The first effect of the large net inflow of pension funds for investment in securities has been to drive up the prices of securities, on the well-known economic principle that any big increase in demand for any commodity (including a security) will cause its price to go up. In the UK, for example, the *Financial Times* Industrial Ordinary Share Index of the prices of leading company shares in the mid-1990s was more than ten times higher than it was in the mid-1970s. Similar increases in securities prices occurred in the US, where funded pension schemes have also been proliferating since the 1970s.

When the price of a security goes up, its yield (that is the ratio of the interest or dividends paid on the security to the market price of the security) comes down. High securities prices therefore make securities cheaper and more attractive ways of raising finance for large companies. While the presumption was that this would give rise to a boom in company investment, what actually happened was that companies have been issuing securities in order to repay bank debt, or as a cheaper and more convenient substitute for bank borrowing. Furthermore, with booming securities markets, governments in the US and UK also found it cheaper to raise finance through those markets, rather than borrowing from banks.

This shift from bank borrowing to securities issue by large companies and governments has had dire consequences for the banking systems in the UK and the US, the countries most affected by this shift. Borrowing by large, financially secure companies, together with government borrowing, constitutes the best part of bank asset (or loan) portfolios. Banks have been forced to engage in more risky business: lending to less financially secure borrowers among smaller and medium-sized companies and governments and companies in developing countries, and trading in financial derivatives (see Chapter 9). While securities markets have done very well out of the funded pensions boom, banks in the US and UK have staggered from one crisis to the next: in Britain in the 1980s the third world debt crisis was followed by over-lending to the property market, leading to its crash in the 1990s. US banks had the third world debt crisis, which coincided with their Savings and Loan Association collapse in the 1980s, and which have been followed by more bad lending to so-called 'emerging markets' in the developing countries and financial derivatives markets.

This disintermediation from the banking system is no less real for being less apparent in bank balance sheets. Large companies have followed governments in replacing their short-term borrowing from banks by issuing short-term company bills or 'paper'. Banks in the USA and the UK are allowed to hold such bills as assets, even though they are not allowed to hold company stocks, except in exceptional circumstances. Thus in practice banks have replaced their loans to large companies with company paper. The problem for banks has been that rising liquidity preference among companies in recent decades (see Chapter 7) has meant that companies maintain and increase their bank deposits and their holdings of company paper. While banks may replace good company loans with company paper, they cannot get the return on company paper that would give them an adequate margin over the interest that they need to pay to keep company deposits. In part this is because since the 1980s large companies (such as General Motors or GEC) have been operating in wholesale money markets as buyers of company paper, pushing down its discount rate on occasion below that for bank bills. The disintermediation problem therefore appears as an absence of opportunities to buy bills or lend to sound borrowers at rates which give a secure margin over deposit rates. As interest margins have narrowed, so banks have sought less reliable fee income from currency trading and derivatives operations.

The proponents of funded pension schemes have argued that the build-up of contributions to those schemes would give companies a source of long-term finance in the capital market for the development of their business. This was supposed to reverse the UK's and the US's dismal record of fixed capital investment: since the 1950s, they have spent the lowest proportion of GDP among the advanced industrialized countries on fixed capital investment. The systematic encouragement, by means of various tax benefits, to employers and employees to opt out of the state earnings-related pensions and into funded company pension schemes began in 1976, in the midst of a debate on the de-industrialization of Britain. More than two decades later, de-industrialization has not been reversed in Britain or the US. On the contrary, the situation has, if anything, got worse, with both countries remaining on a stagnant or only slowly increasing industrial production trend, and experiencing rising deficits in foreign trade in manufacturing goods. The early optimism that cheap, long-term finance would be directed to productive investment has proved illusory. The main reason for this has already been referred to in the first part of this book. Although not difficult to understand, it goes contrary to conventional wisdom in economics: it is that cheaper finance cannot increase the amount of productive investment in an economy, but can substantially reduce it.

Let us consider a company faced with a rising demand for its shares due to the immaturity of funded pension schemes. Its first inclination will be to reduce its interest burden by issuing shares and using the proceeds to repay bank borrowing. This will immediately improve the recorded profitability of its operations as its interest costs are reduced. (According to the canons of accountancy, dividends paid on shares are not costs, so the substitution of dividends for interest reduces costs.) Supposing, though, that demand for its shares still continues to rise. Well, then the company may start to look around for ways in which money raised by issuing more shares might bring more profit to the company. At this point, the company may realize that it can take over an indebted company and use its own share issue to repay the indebted company's borrowing. The company that has been taken over will, through the reduction of its interest costs, appear to be more profitable without any change in its circumstances or management. Of course, this is not an increase in operating profits: it is merely that interest payments are deducted from operating profits to arrive at pre-tax profits, whereas dividends paid on shares are not so deducted. Our company will now join the ranks of successfully growing companies whose expansion thrills the stock market but adds nothing to the productive capacity of the economy. The corporate paragons of the UK and the US, and the largest companies in those countries, have been expanding in precisely this way. Indeed, when they can no longer expand by takeover, companies can still conjure up additional profits by deglomerating: separating out activities into subsidiaries which can replace debt with shares issued in addition to those of the parent company.

Of course, it is quite possible that, in our company, there may be unreconstructed management, Veblen's 'engineers' perhaps, so afflicted with nostalgia for the past glories of their industry that they may actually wish to use an increase in share issue to expand productive capacity by installing new equipment in new factories and employing more workers. Such managers will usually be put right by the finance director of their company. When capital market inflation is depressing fixed capital investment, and by implication real economic activity, most companies would lose less money entrusting it to commodity or derivatives traders than they would by issuing securities to finance fixed capital investment. Assets in financial markets are more liquid than fixed capital. Even if the company may not make any more money out of financial assets, it will certainly see its money more frequently, which is reassuring in uncertain times. Most likely, if the capital market is being systematically inflated, profits can be made from the purchase and sale of financial assets, even if there is no improvement in the productivity of the real assets underlying those financial instruments. Thus, in a period of capital market inflation, engagement with financial novelties passes for 'progressive finance' because of the ease with which such novelties can absorb large quantities of additional capital, in the seemingly profitable ventures admired by the many advocates of innovative financial intermediation. Indeed, since the leaders among those advocates are the brokers and bankers who organize those markets, an interest in progressive finance becomes a prerequisite for the kind of sound reputation that secures a good credit rating and a rising (notional) evaluation for a company's securities.

Moreover, most companies, at most times, are operating with some unused capacity. Only if demand is so buoyant as to use up that capacity is additional capacity likely to be profitable. Even then, fixed capital investment is expensive and risky: if it does not prove to be worthwhile and has to be abandoned, it is unlikely that the sunk costs would be recovered. Most fixed capital is very specific to particular industrial processes and if one company cannot make a profit on the venture, it is not very likely that another company in the same industry would. The company will have lost the money raised, but would still be burdened with the requirement to pay dividends or interest on the securities used to finance the venture. As was argued in Chapter 1, in a market economy companies that invest in fixed capital usually do so out of their own financial reserves, only re-financing their investment in financial markets after it has proven to be a success. In this way they ensure that, if the venture fails, they may have lost money, but the rest of the business would still be a going concern because it has not burdened itself with potentially ruinous financial liabilities. Only small companies and companies in developing countries finance their investments the high-risk way, by raising funds externally.

Precisely because money borrowed, or raised in the securities markets, entails a future financial liability to those markets, such money is best used for short-term, very liquid ventures such as the takeovers described above. The prototype of the successful business of today is a conglomerate like Hanson Trust, GEC, BTR, Trafalgar House. These companies make more money out of buying and selling companies than they do out of productive investment. Even when such companies deglomerate, as happened recently with Imperial Chemicals Industries or Hanson Trust, it is usually to issue additional equity to retire debt. Hence the record of fixed capital investment in the UK and the US remains as dismal as it was before funded pension schemes became widespread. The contribution of funded pension schemes to the corporate economy of the UK and the US has been to inflate capital markets in which unproductive takeover and corporate restructuring activity flourishes, while industrial production and employment activity stagnate.[2]

3.2　Capital market inflation and monetary policy

Among the most notoriously pernicious effects of asset price inflation is that it offers speculators the prospect of gain in excess of the costs of borrowing the money to buy the asset whose price is being inflated. This is how many unstable Ponzi financing structures, which the next section explains, begin. There are usually strict regulations to prevent or limit banks' direct investment in financial instruments without any assured residual liquidity, such as equity or common stocks. However, it is less easy to prevent banks from lending to speculative investors, who then use the proceeds of their loans to buy securities or to limit lending secured on financial assets. Loans secured directly, or indirectly, on stock market assets have been an important factor in the collapse of Japanese banks following the fall in stock market prices during the 1990s. As long as asset markets are being inflated, such credit expansions also conceal from banks, their shareholders and their regulators the disintermediation that occurs when the banks' best borrowers, governments and large companies, use bills and company paper instead of bank loans for their short-term financing. As long as the boom proceeds, banks can enjoy the delusion that they can replace the business of governments and large companies with good lending secured on stocks.

In addition to undermining the solvency of the banking system, and distracting commerce and industry with the possibilities of lucrative corporate restructuring, capital market inflation also tends to make monetary policy ineffective. Monetary policy is conducted by the central bank through operations in banking markets. These are principally the fixing of reserve requirements, buying and selling short-term paper or bills in the money or inter-bank markets, buying and selling government bonds and fixing short-term interest rates. As noted in the previous section, with capital market inflation there has been a proliferation of short-term financial assets traded in the money markets, as large companies and banks find it cheaper to issue their own paper than to borrow for banks. This disintermediation has extended the range of short-term liquid assets which banks may hold. As a result of this it is no longer possible for central banks, in countries experiencing capital market inflation, to control the overall amount of credit available in the economy: attempts to squeeze the liquidity of banks in order to limit their credit advances by, say, open market operations (selling government bonds) are frustrated by the ease with which banks may restore their liquidity by selling bonds or their holdings of short-term paper or bills.[3] In this situation central banks have been forced to reduce the scope of their monetary policy to the setting of short-term interest rates.[4]

Economists have long believed that monetary policy is effective in controlling price inflation in the economy at large, as opposed to inflation of securities prices. Various rationalizations have been advanced for this efficacy of monetary policy. For the most part they suppose some automatic causal connection between changes in the quantity of money in circulation and changes in prices, although the Austrian school of economists tended on occasion to see the connection as being between changes in the rate of interest and changes in prices.[5]

Whatever effect changes in the rate of interest may have on the aggregate of money circulating in the economy, the effect of such changes on prices has to be through the way in which an increase or decrease in the rate of interest causes alterations in expenditure in the economy. Businesses and households are usually hard-headed enough to decide their expenditure and financial commitments in the light of their nominal revenues and cash outflows, which may form their expectations, rather than in accordance with their expectations or optimizing calculations.[6] If the same amount of money continues to be spent in the economy, then there is no effective reason for the business-people setting prices to vary prices. Only if expenditure in markets is rising or falling would retailers and industrialists consider increasing or decreasing prices. The notion, fashionable since the 1970s, that businesspeople are guided in the setting of prices by their *expectations* of price changes elsewhere in the economy is less practical because it requires them to take a view on developments in the rest of the economy, rather than the state of demand and supply in their market. Because price expectations are observable directly with difficulty, they may explain everything in general and therefore lack precision in explaining anything in particular. Notwithstanding their effects on all sorts of expectations, interest rate changes affect inflation directly through their effects on expenditure.

The principal expenditure effects of changes in interest rates occur among net debtors in the economy, i.e., economic units whose financial liabilities exceed their financial assets. This is in contrast to net creditors, whose financial assets exceed their liabilities, and who are usually wealthy enough not to have their spending influenced by changes in interest rates. If they do not have sufficient liquid savings out of which to pay the increase in their debt service payments, then net debtors have their expenditure squeezed by having to devote more of their income to debt service payments. The principal net debtors are governments, households with mortgages and companies with large bank loans.

With or without capital market inflation, higher interest rates have never constrained government spending because of the ease with which governments may issue debt. In the case of indebted companies, the degree to which their expenditure is constrained by higher interest rates depends on their degree of indebtedness, the available facilities for additional financing and the liquidity of their assets.

In the previous section it was pointed out that as a consequence of capital market inflation, larger companies reduce their borrowing from banks because it becomes cheaper and more convenient to raise even short-term finance in the booming securities markets. This then makes the expenditure of even indebted companies less immediately affected by changes in bank interest rates, because general changes in interest rates cannot affect the rate of discount or interest paid on securities already issued. Increases in short-term interest rates to reduce general price inflation can then be easily evaded by companies financing themselves by issuing longer-term securities, whose interest rates tend to be more stable. Furthermore, with capital market inflation, companies are more likely to be over-capitalized and have excessive financial liabilities, against which companies tend to hold a larger stock of more liquid assets.[7] As inflated financial markets have become more unstable, this has further increased the liquidity preference of large companies (see Part III). This excess liquidity enables the companies enjoying it to gain higher interest income to offset the higher cost of their borrowing and to maintain their planned spending. Larger companies, with access to capital markets, can afford to issue securities to replenish their liquid reserves. Thus the high interest rates from 1989 to 1992, which brought about the end of the 1980s boom in the UK, had only a marginal effect on companies' expenditures. Their principal anti-inflationary effect was through the reduced expenditure of households which had entered into very large variable-rate mortgage commitments during the 1980s property boom, and small and medium-sized companies financing themselves with debt. Thus capital market inflation reduced anti-inflationary monetary policy to squeezing the expenditure of households and smaller companies.

If capital market inflation reduces the effectiveness of monetary policy against product price inflation, because of the reduced borrowing of companies and the ability of booming asset markets to absorb large quantities of bank credit, interest rate increases have appeared effective in puncturing asset market bubbles in general and capital market inflations in particular. The inflated Japanese stock and property markets never recovered from the sharp rise in Japanese interest rates in 1991,[8] and rising interest rates may have been a factor in the collapse of the Mexican markets in 1995 and the East Asian markets in 1997.

Whether interest rate rises actually can effect an end to capital market inflation depends on how such rises actually affect the capital market. In asset markets, as with anti-inflationary policy in the rest of the economy, such increases are effective when they squeeze the liquidity of indebted economic units by increasing the outflow of cash needed to service debt payments and by discouraging further speculative borrowing. However, they can only be effective in this way if the credit being used to inflate the capital market is short term or is at variable rates of interest determined by the short-term rate. There is no evidence that short-term borrowing was on a scale commensurate with the emerging market boom and subsequent crises in it. The way in which high short-term interest rates reduce capital market inflation and burst asset price bubbles in general illustrates not so much the efficacy of interest rate policy, as the degree to which capital market inflation undermines any relatively stable relationship between short-term interest rates and capital markets, such as the one implied by the yield curve, or the one made explicit in Keynes's theory of the speculative motive for holding money.

The reader will recall that Keynes's speculative demand for money is the liquidity preference or demand for short-term securities of rentiers in relation to the yield on long-term securities. Keynes's speculative motive is 'a continuous response to gradual changes in the rate of interest'[9] in which, as interest rates along the whole maturity spectrum decline, there is a shift in rentiers' portfolio preference toward more liquid assets. Keynes clearly equated a rise in equity (common stock) prices with just such a fall in interest rates.[10] Arguably, as was noted in Chapter 2, with falling interest rates, the increasing preference of rentiers for short-term financial assets could keep the capital market from excessive inflation.

But the relationship between rates of interest, capital market inflation and liquidity preference is somewhat more complicated. In reality, investors hold liquid assets not only for liquidity, which gives them the option to buy higher-yielding longer-term stocks when their prices fall, but also for yield. During an extended period of high interest rates and liquid financial investment institutions, such as that which has characterized the UK and US economies since 1980, short-term financial assets acquire longer-term investment value. This marginalizes Keynes's speculative motive for liquidity. The motive was based on Keynes's distinction between what he called 'speculation' (investment for capital gain) and 'enterprise' (investment long term for income). In our times, the modern rentier is the fund manager investing long term on behalf of pension and insurance funds and competing for returns against other funds managers. As was noted in the previous chapter, an inflow into the capital markets in excess of the financing requirements of firms and governments results in rising prices and turnover of stock. This higher turnover means greater liquidity so that, as long as the capital market is being inflated, the speculative motive for liquidity is more easily satisfied in the market for long-term securities.

Furthermore, capital market inflation adds a premium of expected inflation, or prospective capital gain, to the yield on long-term financial instruments. Hence when the yield decreases, due to an increase in the securities' market or actual price, the prospective capital gain will not fall in the face of this capital appreciation, but may even increase if it is large or abrupt. Rising short-term interest rates will therefore fail to induce a shift in the liquidity preference of rentiers towards short-term instruments until the central bank pushes these rates of interest above the sum of the prospective capital gain and the market yield on long-term stocks. Only at this point will there be a shift in investors' preferences, causing capital market inflation to cease, or bursting an asset bubble.

This suggests a new financial instability hypothesis, albeit one that is more modest and more limited in scope and consequence than Minsky's Financial Instability Hypothesis.[11] During an economic boom, capital market inflation adds a premium of expected capital gain to the market yield on long-term stocks. As long as this yield plus the expected capital gain exceed the rate of interest on short-term securities set by the central bank's monetary policy, rising short-term interest rates will have no effect on the inflow of funds into the capital market and, if this inflow is greater than the financing requirements of firms and governments, the resulting capital market inflation. Only when the short-term rate of interest exceeds the threshold set by the sum of the prospective capital gain and the yield on long-term stocks will there be a shift in rentiers' preferences. The increase in liquidity preference will reduce the inflow of funds into the capital market. As the rise in stock prices moderates, the prospective capital gain gets smaller, and may even become negative. The rentiers' liquidity preference increases further and eventually the stock market crashes, or ceases to be active in stocks of longer maturities.

At this point, the minimal or negative prospective capital gain makes equity or common stocks unattractive to rentiers at any positive yield, until the rate of interest on short-term securities falls below the sum of the prospective capital gain and the market yield on those stocks. When the short-term rate of interest does fall below this threshold, the resulting reduction in rentiers' liquidity preference revives the capital market.

Thus, in between the bursting of speculative bubbles and the resurrection of a dormant capital market, monetary policy has little effect on capital market inflation. Hence it is a poor regulator for 'squeezing out inflationary expectations' in the capital market.

The case of the capital market inflation produced by the establishment of funded pension schemes is different. The sustained inflation of capital markets by pension funds can maintain a permanently positive prospective capital gain in those markets, putting this monetary capital market cycle into abeyance if short-term interest rates are not raised even higher to counteract this. Moreover, pension funds' purchases of securities are not financed with credit, but through the contributions of employees and companies. Such purchases are therefore largely immune to increases in the rate of interest. Thus, while capital market inflation weakens the influence of monetary policy on the economy in general, because of the reduced dependence of larger borrowers on bank credit, the inflation of capital markets by pension funds renders ineffective attempts at controlling that inflation by increases in interest rates.

3.3 Ponzi finance and securities markets

When funded pension schemes were first put forward at the beginning of the 1970s as a private sector alternative to state earnings-related pensions, the merchant (investment) banks and stockbroking firms that promoted them did not anticipate how successful they would become in that, by the 1990s, pension schemes and allied forms of life assurance would come to own most of the stocks and shares quoted on the world's stock markets. As recently as

1960, the majority of shares (ordinary stocks) quoted on the London Stock Exchange were owned by private individuals. By the 1990s, most of them were owned by pension funds and insurance companies who have thus become the rentiers of our time. In the US, by the mid-1990s, the majority of stocks were owned by pension funds or mutual funds operating pension schemes. This has made a fundamental difference to the way in which these pension funds operate. When pension funds held a minority of stocks, the funds could altogether put money into stock markets by buying stocks, or withdraw it by selling, without significantly affecting prices or the liquidity of the market as a whole. Now that pension funds and allied life assurance and mutual funds constitute the majority of the market, it is not possible for them to withdraw funds altogether without causing a fall in prices, or even a stock market crash.

Because of their success, pension funds have become the newest and possibly the most catastrophic example of Ponzi finance. The term Ponzi finance was invented by the American economist Hyman P. Minsky as part of his analysis of financial market inflation. It describes a form of finance in which new liabilities are issued to finance existing liabilities. According to Minsky, financial crises are caused by the collapse of 'financial structures' whose failure is precipitated by their increasing 'financial fragility'. Financial structures are simply commitments to make payments in the future, against claims that result in incoming payments in the future. For Minsky, the characteristic feature of financial markets and financial speculation is that they afford opportunities for economic units to enter into future financial commitments, in the expectation of gain. In this respect, at least, they are similar to fixed capital investment.[12] Success in securing gains persuades speculators to enter into further commitments, which become more 'fragile', i.e., more prone to collapse because future commitments become more speculative and less covered by assured financial inflows.

Minsky identifies three types of financial commitments, which are distinguished by the different degree of financial risk that they entail. In hedge finance, future commitments are exactly matched by cash inflows. A common example is the practice in banking of lending at variable or floating rates of interest. In this way, if a bank has to pay more interest to its depositors, it can recoup the increase by raising the interest rates that it charges to its borrowers (assuming that its depositors cannot withdraw their deposits before the term of the loan expires).

Speculative finance is characterized by certain commitments which have to be covered by cash inflows which may rise or fall, or uncertain commitments against a fixed cash inflow. If a bank lends money at a fixed rate of interest it is engaging in speculative finance, because it is running the risk that it may have to pay a higher rate of interest to depositors if interest rates rise. However, to set against this risk it has the possibility that the interest rates paid to depositors may fall, and it will thereby make additional gains from a wider margin between lending and borrowing rates.

Ponzi finance, in Minsky's view, is a situation in which both commitments and cash inflows are uncertain, so that there is a possibility of an even more enhanced profit if commitments fall and the cash inflow rises. Against this has to be set the possibility that commitments and the cash inflow will move together so that only a minimal profit will be secured, or that commitments will rise and the cash inflow will fall, in which case a much more serious loss will be entered than would have occurred under speculative finance.

Ponzi finance lies behind the view that is no less erroneous for being widely repeated, that a higher return reflects the 'greater risk' of an enterprise. This is exemplified in the practice of banks charging higher rates of interest for what they perceive as greater risks. Behind this view lies the Austrian tradition, from Böhm-Bawerk onwards, of regarding economic outcomes as analogous to the gains and lotteries obtainable from repeated routine games, such as the tossing of a dice. The certain pay-off (or 'certainty-equivalent') is held to be lower than some possible pay-off. The association of the greater pay-off with its lower probability then leads to a presumption that the latter 'causes' the former.[13] However, the profits of companies and financial institutions are not the proceeds of gaming, however much enterprise in an unstable market system may *appear* similar to gambling. In fact, these profits are the outcomes of financial flows that ebb and progress through the economy, propelled by actual expenditure and financing decisions. The systems of financial claims and liabilities arising from those decisions become more fragile, as first speculative and then Ponzi financing structures come to predominate, and larger gains and larger losses may then be made. But the possibility of extraordinary profits or losses in Ponzi financing structures in no way means that realization of such profits is caused or justified by the possibility of the losses. Ponzi finance arises out of objective contractual obligations. The 'greater risk', which is held to justify a higher cost of finance, may be entirely subjective or a cover for monopoly profits in finance.

The simplest example of Ponzi finance is borrowing money to pay interest on a loan. In this case, the financial liability is increased, with no reduction in the original loan. Pyramid bank deposit schemes were the schemes after which this phenomenon is named, and they are perhaps the most extreme example of such financial structures. In a pyramid deposit scheme, the financier might take, say, £100 from a depositor, and promise to double this money after a month if the depositor introduces two new depositors at the end of that month. The two new depositors get the same terms and when they pay in their £100 respectively, £100 goes to double the money of the first depositor, and the other £100 is the financier's profit. The two new depositors get their profit at the end of the next month from the new deposits paid in by the four new depositors that they introduce to the scheme, and so on. Initially, such schemes promise and deliver good profits. But their flaw lies in the fact that they require deposits to rise exponentially in order to pay the promised rewards to depositors. In the example that is described above, deposits have to double each month so that after one year, the scheme requires £409,600 in deposits just to keep solvent. After the thirteenth month, £819,200 would need to be deposited to keep up promised payments to depositors. Such schemes therefore usually collapse when they run out of gullible people to deposit their savings in them. While their life can be briefly extended by persuading depositors not to withdraw their profits, this cannot work for more than one or two payment periods, because such schemes are so dependent on *increasing* amounts of *additional* money being paid into them in each successive period.

Ponzi schemes are named after Charles Ponzi, an Italian immigrant who swindled Boston investors in 1919 and 1920 with a pyramid banking scheme. Minsky noted that Ponzi's scheme 'swept through the working classes and even affected "respectable" folk'.[14] Because they prey on the poor and the ignorant, Ponzi schemes in banking are usually banned, although this does not prevent them from occurring in countries where it is difficult to regulate them. In recent years, Ponzi schemes have surfaced in Portugal and Eastern Europe.

In Minsky's view, financial collapses occur because booms in financial markets result in sufficient profits for speculative and Ponzi finance to induce a shift from hedge finance to speculative and Ponzi finance. Some of the problems with a simplified version of this analysis, in rising indebtedness during an economic boom, were discussed in Chapter 1. In this Part the analysis goes beyond business cycles to examine Ponzi financial structures in capital markets.

Ponzi finance in securities markets is much more common than in banking. Indeed, it is arguable that such finance is essential for the liquidity of markets in long-term securities: if a security is bought, it may have an assured 'residual liquidity' if it is a bond in that, when it matures, the money will then be returned to the investor. If, however, the security is a share (or common stock in the US, or one of the recently fashionable perpetual bonds) which is not repaid by the issuer except on liquidation of the company, then it has no assured residual liquidity. Its liquidity (i.e., the possibility of obtaining the money back) depends on some other investor wishing to buy it at a reasonable price. If the share is to be sold at a profit, then the condition for this to happen is that demand for it has risen since it was bought. In this respect, liquidity and capital gains in the markets for long-term securities depend on Ponzi finance. In Chapter 2 it was argued that, with capital market inflation, there is a shift to this kind of long-term finance.

Ponzi finance was present at the very inception of modern stock markets. The South Sea Company and the Mississippi Company, whose stocks featured in the first stock market collapse of 1720 (see below), both ended up issuing stocks to raise finance in order to buy stocks to keep the market in their stocks liquid and stable. In modern times, this is a common feature of merger and takeover activity in capital markets. Corporate takeovers are frequently financed by issuing securities. The proceeds of the new issue are used to buy in the target company's stock 'at a premium', i.e., at a price that is greater than the pre-takeover market price. The money raised by issuing the new stocks is used to pay the higher return to the stock-holders of the company being taken over. In this case, issuing new stock is exactly equivalent to the pyramid banking practice of taking in new deposits in order to pay an enhanced return to older depositors, which is the premium on the target company's stock. The main difference between the two types of operation is that, during such takeover activity, the stock market as a whole functions as a pyramid banking scheme. However, precisely because it is the market *as a whole* which is operating in this Ponzi way, the pyramid nature of the venture is less obvious, and the gains are greater, because more and wealthier contributors are involved. Since this is an outcome of the normal functioning of the market, which may hitherto have been acting in a perfectly proper and respectable fashion, raising finance for industry and providing for widows and orphans, it is not possible to 'finger' the perpetrator of the pyramid scheme.

A more obviously controversial kind of Ponzi finance is the practice known as 'ramping' the market. A financier discreetly buys up a particular stock over a period of time, and then announces with great fanfare that he or she is buying in the stock. There are few markets in which emulatory competition is as strong as financial markets, where being conservative in practice and faddish in innovation are preconditions for a 'sound' reputation. The 'sounder' that reputation, the more likely it is other investors will imitate the buying strategy. Indeed, there is an element of compulsion about it, depending on the reputation of the investor. Those investors without reputation must follow for whatever reasons the investment direction signalled by investors with reputation, or else languish among lower-growth stocks. As the price of the stock rises due to the increased demand for it, such reputable financiers quietly sell out at a profit to their imitators, thereby confirming their reputation for financial 'soundness'. Obviously, the better the reputation of the financier, the greater the gain from such an operation. To support such a reputation and legitimize the profits from trading on it, financiers will obviously attribute the gains from this practice to their own financial acumen, rather than confessing to having ramped the market.

The almost instantaneous dissemination of relevant information on which modern financial markets pride themselves (and which many financial economists believe makes them near perfect), also facilitates this kind of market manipulation. In securities markets, the investors emulating the financier are the equivalent of the new depositors. They too may make money, if they too can persuade subsequent new investors to buy at higher prices. As with the pyramid banking case, ramping markets depends on *increasing* interest by *additional* investors. Because in practice it is indistinguishable from normal trading (unlike pyramid banking, which is rather more obvious), and because any losers usually have other wealth to fall back on, such practices are frowned upon in securities markets, but cannot be eliminated. However, in the case of pension funds, the eventual losers will be ordinary working people, who will only have a minimal state pension in the future to fall back on. This makes it all the more important to understand how a reputable system for financing pensions has become a Ponzi finance scheme which will in future collapse.

Pension funds in the US and UK have become heavily involved in such Ponzi finance because of their large holdings of long-term securities. Most of the assets of UK and US pension funds consist of irredeemable shares. This contrasts with the practice in more regulated countries, such as Germany, where pension funds are supposed to match the term of their assets to that of their liabilities, i.e., bonds are purchased that mature as the pension fund's pension payments are due. (Such maturity matching is also a way of inducing pension funds to hold large quantities of government bonds.) Before funded pension schemes came to dominate the world's financial markets, it was easy to overlook the fundamental flaw in them, namely that synchronized buying and selling in securities markets by a group of large institutions can affect prices and liquidity in the markets for long-term securities. Even today, most finance students are still taught that the market price of a security depends either on the actual and expected profits of the company issuing the security or on recent changes in that price, and that the liquidity of a financial market (or the possibility of selling securities in it) depends on the number of investors trading in them. In this way these students, and their teachers, are induced to forget what they were taught in elementary micro-economics, namely that the price and liquidity of a commodity depends on supply and demand in the market. This is because modern finance theory starts out from the assumption that markets are so perfectly competitive that the supply of stocks and the demand for them will not make any significant difference to the price or liquidity of a stock and that price changes will sooner or later bring the market into equilibrium. Yet, as was argued in Chapter 2, if, on balance, there is money coming into the market and the majority of traders want to buy, then the price and liquidity of stocks will go up. If, on balance, investors are withdrawing money from the market, then prices will fall, and stocks will become illiquid (i.e., it will become difficult to sell because of an absence of buyers).

After a discussion of privatization Chapter 5 argues that pension funds initially place large contributions surpluses into the capital markets, which is how they have come to dominate them, but that those surpluses are inevitably diminishing. Chapter 6 discusses reasons for expecting future withdrawals by pension funds from capital markets.

4 Capital market inflation and privatization

In the previous chapter it was argued that the inflation of capital markets by pension fund surpluses causes a disintermediation of banking markets by making securities markets cheaper and more convenient sources of finance. The issuing of securities to replace bank debt has therefore been a feature of US and UK markets since the 1970s. However, the pension fund surpluses are in fact revenue foregone by the previous pay-as-you-go systems of pension finance (in which current employees directly pay for current pensions). The counterpart of these surpluses is therefore a deficit of the previous pay-as-you-go system, obliged to maintain pension entitlements to pensioners under the old system, while deprived of contributions from current workers and their employers, now making their contributions to the new funded schemes. The obvious and first solution to this, until the 1980s, would have been to finance the pay-as-you-go deficit with government bonds sold to the new and immature pension funds.

In 1984, the Conservative government in Britain pioneered an apparently new form of finance, with the sale to financial investors of shares in the previously nationalized British Telecom company. This was a huge success, especially when the managers of the sale gave individual private investors priority in the allocation of the new shares, causing institutional investors (primarily pension and insurance funds) to bid up the price of the new shares in the stock market in order to acquire their desired portfolio allocation. This issue of shares was followed by the privatization of the main state industries in the UK. Since then, in Britain, the vast bulk of additional finance raised in the stock market (i.e., funds raised in addition to those used to replace debt) have been privatization issues. This apparent success caught the imaginations of those politicians, economists and financiers who regard the private sector of the post-war mixed economy as the most dynamic element of the economy, and who consider that its lack of vigour since the 1960s has been due to the financial burden of a public sector bloated by its industrial undertakings. The fall of communism in Eastern Europe and the financial problems of developing countries have all been held to be a clear vindication of this view. The multilateral agencies responsible for coordinating economic policies in various countries, the International Monetary Fund (IMF), the

International Bank for Reconstruction and Development (the World Bank), the European Bank for Reconstruction and Development, and the Organization for Economic Co-operation and Development, have all adopted privatization as a key feature of their recommendations for 'sound' economic policies.[1] It forms a crucial part of the 'structural adjustment' which the IMF and the World Bank enforce on countries to which they lend.

Privatization has generated a whole literature on industrial competition and pricing, based largely on the presumed benefits of *laisser-faire* and the efficacy of price controls. These arguments are beyond the scope of a book concerned with financing structures. In this section, privatization is examined as a 'financial circuit' giving rise to a very particular Ponzi structure of financial claims and liabilities. We may start off with the simple observation that when a government issues a bond to finance its activities, the bond is a future financial liability for the government, against which it has the funds raised by the bond. When a government sells a state enterprise into the private sector by issuing shares on the stock market, the financial effect is exactly the same as issuing bonds with one exceptional feature. Funds are raised for the government, but the shares or stocks sold are a future financial liability of the company privatized rather than of the government. In this way the financial manoeuvre is performed of generating funds for the government by stock issues which are claims not against the government but against commercial companies.[2]

This system of privatization is a form of Ponzi finance because it depends on the willingness of investors to purchase claims against private companies with money that is not used to increase the future revenue-generating capabilities of the companies concerned, but is used to finance government expenditure. In a situation of capital market inflation through pension fund surpluses, it is not difficult to find investors willing to buy such stocks. The problem with this kind of finance is that, like Ponzi financing schemes in general, it can only have a temporary success in obtaining finance. When a government runs out of apparently profitable companies to sell, it can no longer raise finance in this way. Hence the financial embarrassment of the Labour government in Britain which, having embraced privatization, came to power in May 1997 after the profitable state companies had been sold. The government of the US has experienced a different kind of financial embarrassment due to the paucity in that country of state enterprises capable of being sold to private investors. In post-communist Eastern Europe, with huge state industries, the problem has been a shortage of willing investors capable of giving money to the government in exchange for state enterprises, and then putting additional money into the enterprise to finance their re-equipment.[3]

The amount of finance which a government can raise in this way is therefore constrained by the number of commercial enterprises at the government's disposal, and the flow of excess funds into the capital market i.e., the degree of capital market inflation. In a situation of capital market inflation, the actual or potential profitability of the companies concerned becomes a lesser consideration as the capital gain (the increase in the value of the stock) constitutes a larger, or even the bulk of the return on investing in the privatization stocks. Nevertheless, the actual profitability of the companies concerned may be affected by the way in which privatization influences government expenditure.

The connection between government expenditure and the profits earned by companies is given by the flow of funds identity.[4] According to this, the net inflow of funds into the industrial and commercial sector of an economy (i.e., its financial accumulation, or gross profits) in a given period is equal to that sector's gross investment in fixed capital and stocks of raw materials and finished and unfinished goods, plus the government's fiscal deficit (its expenditure minus its revenue), plus the trade surplus of the economy (exports minus imports) plus the household sector deficit.[5] The transfer of the ownership of state companies to private ownership does not, by that act, change investment, the trade surplus or the household deficit. However, it does put more money at the disposal of the government. The proceeds of privatization may be used either to reduce the government's borrowing, or to finance additional expenditure. If privatization is solely used to reduce the government's borrowing, so that the balance between expenditure and revenue remains exactly as it would have been without the privatization, then that privatization has no effect on the inflow of funds into, or the profits of, the business sector. All that happens is that the new stock of the company appears in the capital market to replace the government bonds that would otherwise have been issued to finance the fiscal deficit. Such privatization merely transforms government liabilities into corporate liabilities without actually putting any money into the companies that have been privatized. With unchanged profits and a higher stock market capitalization, the earnings per share (i.e., pre-tax profits per share) of listed companies on average will fall.

If, however, the proceeds of privatization are used for additional government expenditure, then this will appear as an increase in the fiscal deficit without any increase in actual government borrowing. The larger fiscal deficit will result in a greater financial inflow or higher gross profits in the corporate sector, as savings are mobilized and circulated through the real economy. It should be noted that the commercial corporate sector has been increased in size by the transfer of the formerly government companies to the private sector. The liabilities to the capital market of the commercial corporate sector have also been increased by the issue of the new privatization stocks (here, as argued in Chapter 1, modern equity shares or common stocks may be treated as liabilities of the companies issuing them). To service the additional liabilities with dividend payments, and avoid the running down of reserves, higher corporate operating profits are necessary in proportion to the increase in liabilities. This argument suggests that, in the absence of an increase in corporate capital investment, the trade surplus or the household deficit, an effective way to increase those profits is to increase government expenditure without raising additional revenue. Indeed, it could be argued that it is the least that the government can do for having saddled the corporate sector with the liabilities for its expenditure, while denying the privatized companies the proceeds of their issue of privatization stocks in the capital market.

The political and financial promoters of privatization in Britain were quick to claim the credit for pioneering what they have regarded as an entirely new method of raising government finance and rolling back the frontiers of state involvement in industry. However, this policy is not new and emphasis on its novelty conceals the financial consequences of earlier privatizations. In 1717, a Scottish adventurer, John Law, was given permission by the Duc d'Orléans, the Regent of France during the minority of Louis XV, to establish the Company of the West (Compagnie d'Occident).[6] The company was given extensive trade monopolies in the French colony of Louisiana, which covered an area of the present-day United States much greater than the present Louisiana. Following a series of takeovers, a large holding company commonly known as the Mississippi Company was established. In the autumn of 1719, the company was given additional rights to issue shares. The money raised from the new issues was used to repay French government bonds and pay government annuities, a financial burden bequeathed to the French state by the wars and magnificence of the Sun King Louis XIV. In return, the holding company was given extensive trading monopolies, minting rights and tax farms from Senegal to Louisiana. This 'privatization' was therefore of the first type described above, i.e., it involved replacing debt by the obligations of the new company, without increasing government expenditure.

The success of the Mississippi Company invited emulation, even in the country which was to pioneer capital markets, England. The South Sea Company, which had been formed in 1711 to exploit trading monopolies in the South Seas, granted by the Crown, started to issue additional shares. In 1720, following the huge and apparent success of the Mississippi Company in relieving the debts and financial obligations of the French government, the South Sea Company was allowed to take over the major share of the British national debt. As in France, the possibilities for managing government debts bloated by the expensive War of Spanish Succession from 1702 to 1713, gave the company an influence out of all proportion to its actual trading prospects. The Bank of England, which had been established in 1694 to manage the government's debt, gave important support and an aura of respectability which common stock promoters lack.[7]

Both the Mississippi Company and the South Sea Company pioneered a prototype of privatization in France and Britain. They collapsed in 1720, not because of that aspect of their activities, but because they became in effect pyramid banking operations, with new finance being raised to finance the buying in of stock to support its price.[8] Had the proceeds of selling government stocks to these companies been used for additional expenditure, creating business and profits for French and British companies, the companies may perhaps have obtained some increase in profits if an unfortunate sense of geography (otherwise so apt for arousing imagined prospects of gain) had not placed their main trading operations in areas where the French and the British governments were not spending money. This may have enabled them to support a more modest stock issue. But insofar as financial success breeds excess, such a policy may merely have encouraged an even greater stock issue and an even more calamitous subsequent collapse.

The fact that these companies promoted a form of privatization does not of course mean that the privatized companies of the 1990s are similar Ponzi structures. Arguably, the latter have been far more careful in their issue of stock. Although Ponzi elements are present in all financial inflations, successive inflations are different. The change of economic circumstances and financial innovation alter the form of financing arrangements as well as justifying that sanguine optimism which reassures the participants in capital market inflation and the construction of fragile financial structures. The essential difference between today's privatizations and those of the Mississippi and South Sea Companies is that Ponzi structures were developed in those companies themselves. At the end of the twentieth century, the Ponzi structure lies not in the privatized companies but in the capital markets and the pension funds that have effectively bought the privatized companies.

There are of course other peripheral Ponzi elements apparent in both cases. Similar tactics have also been used in the two privatization periods to create a second class of investors willing to pay a premium to the first buyers of new stock, by limiting entitlements to the stock on issue. The premium paid to the first owners of stock attracts more demand, even though the premium is only temporary until those excluded from the first stock allocation have secured their desired shares. Law did this at the height of the Mississippi Company mania by limiting new share issues to existing stockholders: what would nowadays be called a Rights Issue, while making sure that plenty of credit for buying the stock was available from his Banque Royale.[9] In the privatizations of the 1980s and 1990s, individual investors have been given preferential initial share allocations, forcing large and liquid investing institutions to bid up the price when the secondary markets in the new stocks opened. In both cases, capital market inflation has been the financial precondition for privatization.

5 Pension fund inflows and their investment

5.1 The cash inflow into pension funds

The crucial issue for financial markets today is whether the pension funds that dominate those markets are buying or selling. This affects the market as a whole, and the markets for individual stocks. Some indication of whether they are buying or selling may be obtained by looking at the cash inflow into pension funds and allied investment funds. This cash inflow is made up of the contributions to pension funds, plus the investment income that is not paid out as pensions. Such additions to their funds are then used to buy securities, stocks and shares, which will then be used to pay the pensions 'funded' in this way.

Whether pension funds are net buyers or net sellers of securities overall depends on their 'maturity'. An 'immature fund' is one in which the inflow of contributions exceeds the outflow of pensions payments. The excess contributions are then invested in financial securities. A 'mature pension fund' is one in which the pensions paid out exceed the amount of contributions. The excess pensions are then paid out of the investment income of the fund, and by selling the securities in the fund. In a steadily growing economy, in which pensionable employment is rising, funded pension schemes may never mature, unless companies close down. In that case the pensions are safe, because they are 'funded' and other funds will obtain additional contributions as the workers transfer employment.

Table 5.1 shows net changes in cash inflows of pension funds and insurance companies in Japan, the US and the UK. Figures for pension funds and insurance companies are usually combined like this because their investment portfolios jointly dominate the world's capital markets and because most insurance companies nowadays provide commercial pension arrangements. Indeed, as the slow-down of economic growth in the advanced industrialized countries since 1990 has reduced the profits from underwriting insurance business in those countries, so their pensions business has become their most profitable activity.

Table 5.1 reveals that the net inflow of funds into pension and insurance funds (i.e., investment income plus contributions and premiums, less

Table 5.1 The contractual saving of the labour force in Japan, the US and UK 1982–95 (% increases throughout)

	Change in employment			Change in net inflows into pension and insurance funds		
	US	*UK*	*Japan*	*US*	*UK*	*Japan*
1982	−0.8	−1.8	1.0	22.4	13.7	15.1
1983	1.3	−1.2	1.7	8.6	7.3	8.4
1984	4.1	2.6	0.6	7.1	24.7	16.6
1985	2.0	1.3	0.7	37.7	1.0	31.6
1986	2.2	0.1	0.8	3.8	14.3	49.8
1987	2.6	2.1	1.0	−41.2	9.5	15.3
1988	2.2	3.2	1.7	52.3	−7.7	19.7
1989	2.0	3.0	1.9	3.7	44.5	10.6
1990	0.4	1.0	2.0	−10.6	−6.5	28.5
1991	−0.9	−1.9	1.9	n.a.	11.1	+0.7
1992	0.6	−0.6	1.1	n.a.	−5.0	−6.7
1993	1.4	1.3	0.2	n.a.	6.0	10.4
1994	3.1	2.1	0.0	n.a.	−9.5	10.5
1995	1.4	1.1	0.0	n.a.	29.9	n.a.

Source: OECD *Historical Statistics* and calculations from *Financial Accounts of OECD Countries*, Tables 313F/17, 313F/07 and 313F/21.

payments to pensioners and policyholders) is unstable. In some years there have been large increases. This is apparent for the years 1982, 1985 and 1988 in the US, and 1982, 1984, 1989 and 1995 in the UK. Japan experienced large increases throughout the 1980s and one in 1993. In other years – 1987 and 1990 in the US, 1988, 1990, 1992 and 1994 in the UK, and in the 1990s in Japan, with the exception of 1993 – these funds have experienced decreases. A part of this instability is caused by the bunching of claims against insurance companies, leading to large payments by them to their policyholders. Another part is caused by the business cycle. There is a high positive income elasticity of demand for life assurance because, in recessions, households are less inclined to take out new policies while, in an economic boom, demand for new policies rises more than proportionately. These two circumstances affect the net inflows into insurance funds. A third factor is the change in the value of assets held in securities markets by pension and insurance funds, which is treated for statistical purposes as a money inflow into the funds, even if no money comes in unless the assets are sold. There is a fourth factor which destabilizes inflows into pension funds. This is the balance between contributions and pensions.

The net cash inflow of pension funds consists of investment income plus pension contributions, less pension payments. Leaving aside for the time being investment income, the contributions to a pension fund, and by aggregation to the pension fund system of a country, may be written as a simple proportion, α, of the wage rate during a given period, w_t, times the labour force in that period, L_t. Normal pension fund practice is to make α sufficient, together with investment income, to secure a 'defined benefit' pension (see below). This can be simplified by postulating that the defined benefit is in proportion, π, to the contribution times the number of years' contributions that have been paid into the fund, n. Therefore an equation for the net cash inflow, CI, of a pension fund, excluding investment income, may be written as:

$$CI = \alpha.w_t.L_t - \pi[\alpha.w_t.L_t + \alpha.w_{t-1}.L_{t-2} + \ldots\ldots + \alpha.w_{t-n}.L_{t-n}]$$

or

$$CI = \alpha.w_t.L_t - \pi.\alpha.[\sum_{t-n}^{t} w_t.L_t] \qquad (5.1)$$

The constant π presupposes that the same number of people reach retirement age in each year, spread equally between different lengths of contribution. For example, after operating for two years, half of the pensioners will have contributed for two years, and the other half for one year only. After three years, one-third will have been in the scheme for one year, one-third for two years, and one-third for three years. Whereas α is the contribution rate for the scheme and is fixed in advance, the approximate size of π may be actuarially determined as the ratio of pension contributions in any one year to the pension that it buys, excluding any benefit from investment income. This ratio depends on the expected duration of life after retirement.

Supposing that forty-five years of contributions buys a pension that is fifty per cent of salary for fifteen years, then each year's contribution will have bought one-third (15 divided by 45) times one-half (pension to salary ratio) i.e.,

$$\alpha.\pi.w_t.L_t = (1/6).w_t.L_t$$

or, more generally

$$\alpha.\pi = \frac{\text{Expected length of retirement}}{\text{Expected length of working life}} \times \frac{\text{Pension}}{\text{Salary}}$$

π is therefore the ratio of the expected total pension payments to earnings in work, divided by the contribution rate:

$$\pi = \frac{\text{Expected length of retirement} \times \text{pension}}{\text{Earnings in work}} \ / \ \text{Contribution rate}$$

In the example above, if the contribution rate is 20 per cent of salary, then π is equal to five-sixths.

We may now consider the conditions for a stable net cash inflow into the pension fund. For this inflow to be constant, the change in the contributions inflow (this year's contributions inflow minus last year's inflow) minus the change in the pensions paid (this year's pensions minus last year's pensions) has to equal zero. Taking first differences causes the summation term Σ in equation 5.1 to fall out of the equation. The change in the net cash inflow (CI') becomes:

$$CI' = \alpha.[w_tL_t - w_{t-1}.L_{t-1}] - \pi.\alpha[w_tL_t]$$

The condition for a constant net cash inflow is no change in it. Setting the change in the net cash inflow to zero gives:

$$\alpha.[w_tL_t - w_{t-1}.L_{t-1}] - \pi.\alpha[w_tL_t] = 0$$

or

$$\alpha.[w_tL_t - wt-1.Lt-1] = \pi.\alpha[w_tL_t]$$

α cancels out to give, on rearrangement

$$\pi = \frac{w_tL_t - w_{t-1}.L_{t-1}}{w_tL_t}$$

as the condition for a stable net cash inflow (excluding investment income) into the pension scheme. In other words, to secure a balance between contributions and pensions, it is necessary for π to equal the rate of growth of the wage bill. Since π is defined as the ratio of pensions to earnings divided by the contribution rate, in general *a constant balance between contributions and pension payments requires that the ratio of expected retirement years, times the annual pension, to earnings in work, divided by the contribution rate, must equal the growth rate of the wage bill of the employed labour force in the scheme.*

In the example given above, in which employment service of forty-five years buys a pension of 50 per cent of annual salary for fifteen years, then stable net inflows into the fund would require the rate of increase of the wage bill to be 83 per cent in each year. This is clearly unrealistic, except perhaps in a situation in which earnings inflation far exceeds the increase in the value of pensions.

If the contribution rate is raised to one-third of earnings, this will require a growth rate of earnings of 50 per cent per annum to support a constant net inflow into the scheme. As an additional measure, the ratio of pension to salary may be reduced from half to one-third. This would then require a growth rate of earnings of one-third to balance contributions with earnings. As a further measure, the ratio of expected years in retirement to working life may be reduced from one-third to one-fifth (equivalent to raising the retirement age to 70). The required rate of growth of earnings would then fall to 20 per cent, still a substantial rate of increase.

Therefore, because earnings and employment do not rise so dramatically, except in periods of high wage inflation, the change in the balance between contributions and pensions in a pension scheme is usually negative. When a pension scheme is established it starts off with a relatively high inflow of contributions and current pensions liabilities which are small at first, because the few contributors that retire first of all have short contribution records, and therefore only small pension entitlements. In each successive year another cohort of retiring workers becomes entitled to a larger pension, by reason of their longer contribution record, than each previous year's cohort. The excess of contributions over pensions is therefore large at first, but rapidly falls and may even become negative as the scheme 'matures'.

From the point of view of the financial markets, the cash inflow into an individual fund is less important than the inflow into all pension funds taken together. It is this overall inflow that affects the flow of funds into capital markets, which was argued in Chapter 2 to be the key influence on asset values. There are two ways of stabilizing the net cash inflow into a country's funded pensions as a whole. One is to organize a system of 'serial maturity' and have a new pension scheme started up in each successive year, so that the resulting cash inflow into the schemes, and hence into the financial markets, is more or less average. However, such a solution would require a degree of centralized organization of the setting up of funded pension schemes. This would be contrary to the essential ethos of funding, which is that free capital markets are the best way of applying the nation's savings to productive investment. Moreover, this solution is limited by the number of schemes that may be set up. To achieve full stability, new schemes would have to be established in each successive year until the last pensioner from the first year's retirement cohort dies. This is feasible only in a country with a very large labour force relative to the number of employees in the average pension scheme, such as the US.[1] In a smaller country, such as the UK or one of the continental European countries, such planned serial maturity would require the annual inauguration of much smaller pension funds. Above all, such stabilization of net pension fund inflows would need a prior recognition that large and subsequently declining cash inflows into financial markets may destabilize those markets. Recognition of this problem may also reveal that there are other, more effective ways of organizing a pension scheme.

The second way of preventing an inexorable fall in net pension fund inflows is successively to increase the scope of funded pension schemes. Initially in the UK, funded pension schemes were private pension arrangements additional to the state pension. As these schemes commenced maturing in the 1970s, the scope of the pension schemes was extended to allow the possibility of contracting out of the state earnings-related pension. This gave a boost to pension fund inflows. As this boost started to diminish again in the 1980s, the scope of the funded pension schemes was further extended to allow for contracting out from non-funded occupational pension schemes, principally in the public sector. As net inflows again started to decline in the 1990s, British politicians and financiers are debating the funding of the basic state pension, which could again boost the net inflow into pension funds.

Increases in the scope of funded pension schemes may be visualized as a graph showing net inflows into funded pension schemes over time. The analysis above shows that pension schemes would normally have net contributions declining over time. Increasing the scope of the schemes increases net contributions sharply before they start to decrease again. Over time this gives a saw-toothed effect, so that the decline of net pensions contributions is broken by steep increases as yet another pension or yet another class of pensioner is brought into the funded system. Moreover, the declining trend may even appear to be reversed by inflation which would give an upward slope to the saw-toothed curve. In real terms, however, the secular trend of net pension fund inflows remains negative, even though it is masked, as in Table 5.1 above, by inflation and increases in the scope of the schemes.

5.2 Pension funds and their investment income

The tendency of the net cash inflow into funded pension schemes to decline was already noted twenty years ago by the Wilson Committee.[2] But the implications of this decline for pensions and the stability of the financial system have not been discussed, or even realized, possibly because of a reluctance to contemplate those implications. Another reason may be the tendency to sell such schemes as 'pots of money' or 'retirement accounts', which suggests that the contributions money remains in the fund, multiplying at compound rates of interest and awaiting withdrawal on retirement. This is, of course, far from the truth: contributions payments are exchanged for financial assets issued by governments and companies, who spend the money thus received, retaining the obligation to pay interest but, in the case of shares, or common stocks, no obligation to repay.

Perhaps the main reason for the failure to consider the financial consequences of declining pension fund inflows lies in the way in which pension fund actuaries calculate investment returns on the assets of their funds. This is normally done by extrapolating past returns into the future. Returns consist of two elements: capital gains (the increase in the price of financial assets held in the portfolio) and income (interest or dividends). Capital gains depend on the rising prices in financial asset markets. If those markets are dominated by pension funds, then prices in the markets will depend on the net inflows of contributions into the pension funds. At any one time, a fund's actuary cannot know what will be the weight of other maturing funds in securities markets in successive years in the future. All that he or she can do is to extrapolate, more or less conservatively, past capital gains.

Let us suppose an extreme case in which the only purchasers of financial assets are pension funds. At the time of their inauguration, when the surplus of contributions over pensions is greatest, the largest net purchases of financial assets are made, driving up prices in the markets. In the following year, when slightly smaller net purchases are made prices may rise, but not by as much as in the first year. In each successive year afterwards, price rises and hence capital gains will be less. When the pension funds mature and have to pay pensions in excess of contributions received, so that money has to be taken out of the financial markets, the absence of other purchasers to buy assets from the funds will cause prices to fall and the market will crash.

Thus the value of financial assets in general is not determined by the profitability of the companies issuing those assets, or the productivity of any underlying real capital assets which may be among the counterparts, in the balance sheets of listed companies, of those companies' financial liabilities. Such profitability may be among the subjective factors in the minds of investment fund managers and may affect their choice of stock, given the amount of funds to be invested. As was argued in Chapters 1 and 2, the general level of financial asset prices is determined by the availability of a purchaser and the price which he or she is prepared to pay for the asset. The only exceptions to this are assets with an immediate residual liquidity, such as bonds due to be repaid by their issuer which have their repayment value fixed by the terms of their issue. But between a half and two-thirds of pension fund assets in the UK and US are held in equity (common stock) without such residual liquidity. Accordingly, financial markets dominated by pension funds holding the majority of their assets in irredeemable securities will have their assets' prices largely determined by the net inflows of funds into those pension funds. In principle, if pension fund net contribution inflows are 'saw-toothed' over time (see previous section) then one would expect stock prices also to fluctuate in a 'saw-toothed' way. In practice, however, the relationship between these net contribution inflows and stock prices is complicated by two factors.

The first of these complicating factors is international diversification. From 1979 in the UK, and during the 1980s in other countries, exchange controls over capital movements have been removed, so that a proportion of the pension fund inflows has been used to purchase foreign securities. If increases in net contributions inflows are invested abroad, and decreases are accommodated by reductions in portfolio investment abroad, the overall effect will be to stabilize the domestic stock market. By the early 1990s 10 per cent of the assets of the world's 500 largest insurance companies and pension funds were invested in foreign securities.[3] During the 1970s, when capital controls prevented the purchase of foreign securities, the proportion of such securities in those portfolios was much lower. To have reached a proportion

Table 5.2 Selected world stock market indices (domestic currency, 1980 = 100)

	US	UK	Japan	Germany	Singapore	Hong Kong
1983	256.5	97.3	128.2	103.3	164.8	85.0
1984	253.8	119.9	153.8	115.7	168.5	91.7
1985	286.1	140.9	182.8	158.3	139.3	157.6
1986	386.3	180.6	238.4	225.9	131.7	176.7
1987	490.1	224.5	337.1	198.2	203.9	266.8
1988	443.7	203.2	393.4	162.9	180.4	233.9
1989	540.2	249.8	495.8	205.0	232.5	256.1
1990	577.3	245.4	429.4	236.3	251.3	277.7
1991	631.1	269.5	354.1	209.7	258.0	347.8
1992	707.5	273.9	264.9	207.7	259.9	501.3
1993	769.3	326.3	280.4	230.2	348.7	722.6
1994	816.8	339.4	289.7	257.1	406.3	845.4
1995	967.6	352.3	253.0	252.5	382.7	912.2

Source: Author's calculations from National Westminster Bank, *Economic and Financial Outlook*, various issues.

of 10 per cent by the 1990s would have required over 10 per cent of net contributions and premium inflows to have been invested abroad.

The second complicating factor is portfolio switches between different markets. These are subject to the vagaries of estimates of future returns, exchange rate projections, and fads among fund managers. Furthermore, on at least two occasions, in October 1987 following the stock market crash that year, and in 1994, after the Mexican financial market collapse, portfolio managers sold foreign stocks and repatriated their proceeds. This affects prices in particular countries' financial markets. While the general level of asset prices in markets dominated by pension funds reflects global pension fund net contribution inflows, changes in the level of prices in particular markets may diverge substantially from changes in those inflows. The stock market price indices in Table 5.2 therefore only broadly follow pension fund inflows.

Among the larger stock markets whose price indices are shown in Table 5.2, two stand out as having the prices of their representative stocks rising almost ten times over the fifteen years since 1980. These are the US market (the above index is taken from the Dow Jones Industrial Stock index of stocks traded in the New York Stock Exchange) and Hong Kong (the table shows the main Hang Seng index). Prices in the US market have grown because this market benefits directly from the investment of the collective savings of the largest economy in the world. As the most powerful capitalist economy, whose dollar currency is the main reserve currency of the world and whose investment institutions dominate international finance, the US also attracts portfolio investment from other countries, and offers more secure markets for funds when other markets are in trouble. (This is further discussed below.)

Prices have risen almost as fast in Hong Kong as in the US. There are specific political and financial reasons for this: 'patriotic' investment by Chinese financial institutions keen to show their approval of Hong Kong's return to Chinese rule, and the position of Hong Kong markets as more accessible markets for Chinese securities whose trade is more strictly controlled in China proper. There have also been some capital outflows from China into the less regulated Hong Kong markets.[4] But the more general factor behind the Hong Kong market's superior performance is its status as an emerging or, more generally, a 'peripheral' market.

5.3 Peripheral and integrated markets

'Peripheral' markets may be defined as markets which generate only a small proportion of their financial inflows from local business and investors, but which attract the interest of 'global' investors. Emerging markets and markets for financial exotica such as financial derivatives are examples of such peripheral markets. Because emerging markets are largely dependent upon attracting international funds in order to generate increases in securities prices and capital gains which will attract further funds, they are particularly good examples of the principles of Ponzi finance at work in securities markets.

A common characteristic feature of peripheral markets is that they have no history of returns to financial investment on the scale on which finance is drawn to those markets in a time of capital market inflation. Such returns in the future have to be inferred on the basis of conjecture and fragmentary information. Investment decisions are therefore more dependent on sentiment, rather than reason. Any optimism is quickly justified by the rapid increase in asset prices in response to even a modest excess net inflow of money into such a market.

Emerging markets illustrate this very clearly. Such markets exist in developing and semi-industrialized countries with relatively undeveloped pensions and insurance institutions, principally because only a small proportion of households earn enough to be able to put aside long-term savings. The first fund manager comes upon such a market in the conviction that a change of government or government policy, or some temporary change in commodity prices, has opened a cornucopia of profitable opportunities and therefore warrants the dismissal of a history of economic, financial and political instability. If he or she is able with buying and enthusiasm to attract other speculators and fund managers to enter the market, they may drive up asset prices and make the largest capital gains. The second and third fund managers to buy into that market also make capital gains. The emulatory competition of trading on reputation[5] while competing for returns makes international investment managers especially prone to this kind of 'herd' investment.

For a while such capital inflows into the market make everyone happy: international fund managers are able to show good returns from the funds in their care; finance theorists can reassure themselves that greater financial risks *are* compensated by higher returns; the government of the country in which the emerging market is located can sell its bonds and public sector enterprises to willing foreign investors and use the proceeds to balance its budget and repay its debts; the watchdogs of financial prudence in the International Monetary Fund can hail the revival of finance, the government's commitment to private enterprise and apparent fiscal responsibility; state enterprises, hitherto stagnating because of under-investment by over-indebted governments, suddenly find themselves in the private sector commanding seemingly limitless opportunities for raising finance; the country's currency after years of depreciation acquires a gilt-edged stability as dollars (the principal currency of international investment) flow in to be exchanged for local currency with which to buy local securities; the central bank accumulates dollars in exchange for the local currency that it issues to enable foreign investors to invest in the local markets and, with larger reserves, secures a new ease in managing its foreign liabilities; the indigenous middle and professional classes who buy financial and property (real estate) assets in time for the boom are enriched and for once cease their perennial grumbling at the sordid reality of life in a poor country. In this conjuncture the most banal shibboleths of enterprise and economic progress under capitalism appear like the very essence of worldly wisdom.

Only in such a situation of capital market inflation are the supposed benefits of foreign direct investment realized. Such investment by multinational companies is widely held to improve the 'quality' or productivity of local labour, management and technical know-how in less developed countries, whose technology and organization of labour lags behind that of the more industrialized countries.[6] But only the most doltish and ignorant peasant would not have his or her productivity increased by being set to work with a machine of relatively recent vintage under the guidance of a manager familiar with that machine and the kind of work organization that it requires. It is more doubtful whether the initial increase in productivity can be realized without a corresponding increase in the export market (developing countries have relatively small home markets). It is even more doubtful if the productivity increase can be repeated without the replacement of the machinery by even newer machinery.

The favourable conjuncture in the capital markets of developing countries can be even more temporary. There are limits on the extent to which even private sector companies may take on financial liabilities and privatization is, as we saw in Chapter 4, merely a system for transferring such liabilities from the government to the private sector without increasing the financial resources of the companies privatized. But to sustain capital gains in the emerging stock market, additional funds have to continue to flow in buying new liabilities of the government or the private sector, or buying out local investors. When new securities cease to attract international fund managers, the inflow stops. Sometimes this happens when the government privatization drive pauses, because the government runs out of attractive state enterprises or there are political and procedural difficulties in selling them. A fall in the proceeds from privatization may reveal the government's underlying fiscal deficit, causing the pundits of international finance to sense the odour of financial unsoundness. More commonly (for example, in Mexico in 1994 and the Far East in 1997) rising imports and general price inflation, due to the economic boom set off by the inflow of foreign funds, arouse just such an odour in the noses of those pundits. Such financial soundness is a subjective view. Even if nothing is wrong in the country concerned, the prospective capital gain and yield in some other market need only rise above the expected inflation and yield of the country, to cause a capital outflow which will usually be justified in retrospect by an appeal to perceived, if not actual, financial disequilibrium.

Ponzi financial structures are characterized by ephemeral liquidity. At the time when money is coming into the markets they appear to be just the neoclassical ideal of market perfection, with lots of buyers and sellers scrambling for bargains and arbitrage profits. At the moment when disinvestment takes hold the true nature of peripheral markets and their ephemeral liquidity is revealed as trades which previously sped through in the frantic paper chase for profits are now frustrated. This too is particularly apparent in emerging markets. In order to sell, a buyer is necessary. If the majority of investors in a market also wish to sell, then sales cannot be executed for want of a buyer and the apparently perfect market liquidity dries up. The crash of the emerging stock market is followed by the fall in the exchange value of the local currency. Those international investors that succeeded in selling now have local currency which has to be converted into dollars if the proceeds of the sale are to be repatriated, or invested elsewhere. Exchange through the local banking system may now be frustrated if it has inadequate dollar reserves: a strong possibility if the central bank has been using dollars to service foreign debts. In spite of all the reassurance that this time it will be different because capital inflows are secured on financial instruments issued by the private sector, international investors are at this point as much at the mercy of the central bank and the government of an emerging market as international banks were at the height of the sovereign debt crisis of the 1980s. Moreover, the greater the success of the peripheral market in attracting funds, and hence the greater the boom in prices in that market, the greater is the desired outflow when it comes. With the fall in liquidity of financial markets in developing countries comes a fall in the liquidity of foreign direct investment, making it difficult to secure appropriate local financial support or repatriate profits.[7]

Another factor which contributes to the fragility of peripheral markets is the opaqueness of financial accounting in them, in the sense that however precise and discriminating may be the financial accounting conventions, rules and reporting, they do not provide accurate indicators of the financial prospects of particular investments. In emerging markets this is commonly supposed to be because they lack the accounting regulations and expertise which supports the sophisticated integrated financial markets of the industrialized countries. In those industrialized countries, where accounting procedures are supposed to be much more transparent, peripheral markets such as venture capital and financial futures still suffer from accounting inadequacies because financial innovation introduces liabilities that have no history and which are not included in conventional accounts (notably the so-called 'off-balance sheet' liabilities). More important than these gaps in financial reporting is the volatility of profits from financial investment in such peripheral markets, and the absence of any stable relationship between profits from trading in their instruments and the previous history of those instruments or the financial performance of the company issuing them. Thus, even where financial records are comprehensive, accurate and revealed, they are a poor indicator of prospective returns from investments in the securities of peripheral markets.

With more than usually unreliable financial data, trading in those markets is much more based on reputation than on any systematic financial analysis: the second and third investor in such a market is attracted by the reputation of the first and subsequently the second investor. Because of the direct connection between financial inflows and values in securities markets, the more trading takes place on the basis of reputation the less of a guide to prospective returns is afforded by financial analysis. Peripheral markets are therefore much more prone to 'ramping' than other markets.[8]

Why would such a crisis of withdrawal not occur, at least not on such a scale, in the more locally integrated capital markets of the advanced industrialised countries? First of all, integrated capital markets such as those of the UK, Japan and the US are the domestic base for international investors. In periods of financial turbulence, they are more likely to have funds repatriated to them than to have funds taken out of them. For example, during the 1987 Crash, which affected a number of financial centres, those in the largest economies of the world were least affected by the Crash. More peripheral stock markets suffered the worst falls in prices and market breakdowns.[9]

Second, institutional investors tend to be more responsive to pressure to be 'responsible investors' in their home countries. In large measure this is because home securities make up the vast majority of investment fund portfolios. Ultimately, investment institutions will use their liquidity to protect the markets in which most of their portfolio is based. For example, in 1987, Japanese brokers heeded Finance Ministry requests to buy stock on the day of the Crash. The 'responsibility' of Japanese insurance and pension funds did not stop there. These funds were also active in buying stock in London and New York, ensuring the smooth recovery of those markets from the Crash.[10]

Finally, the locally integrated markets of the advanced industrialized countries have investing institutions with far greater wealth than the developing or semi-industrialized countries. Those markets are home for the pension funds which dominate the world markets. Among their wealth are deposits and other liquid assets which may be easily converted to support a stock market by buying securities. The poorer countries of the world have even poorer pension funds, which could not support their markets against an outflow due to portfolio switches by international investors.

The location of the world's major pension and insurance funds in the main financial centres of the industrialized countries also explains the strong rise of the US capital markets during the 1990s, at a time when inflows of additional investable funds into pension and insurance funds was stagnant or falling (see Tables 5.1 and 5.2). Those funds' investment managers respond to crisis in peripheral markets by 'repatriating' funds to more stable markets at home. Fund managers are more familiar with these markets, where capital values have a more 'supportive' institutional environment, than peripheral markets, and investment in them is less subject to exchange rate fluctuation. Brought to their home country, pension fund investments may avoid the effects of exchange rate fluctuations entirely. Successive crises in Mexico in 1994, derivatives markets in 1995 and 1996, and in Malaysian, Indonesian and Thai financial markets in 1997 gave rise to successive shifts in funds to concentrate portfolios more on capital markets in the United States.[11] Indeed, the Mexican crisis was precipitated by such a capital outflow for months before the crisis actually broke out in December 1994.

Thus integrated markets are more 'secure' in that they are less prone to collapse than emerging or, more generally, peripheral markets. But precisely because of the large amount of trade already concentrated in the integrated markets, prices in them are much less likely to respond to investment fund inflows from abroad. In general, the capital markets of Japan, the US and the UK have benefited most from inflows into funded pension schemes since the 1970s, and therefore have enjoyed a more secure upward trend in prices. Pension and insurance fund practice is to extrapolate those capital gains into the future for the purposes of determining the solvency of those funds. However, those gains were obtained because of a combination of inflation, the increased scope of funded pensions and the flight of funds from peripheral markets. For the reasons given in this chapter and Chapter 6, it is unlikely that these inflows will be sustained in the future, and hence that past performance will be a good guide to future price trends.

6   The end of funded pension schemes

6.1 The limits of capital market inflation

In Chapter 5 it was argued that a funded pension scheme has a tendency to diminishing net contributions inflows because, as more and more employees with longer and longer pensionable service reach retirement, the fund's payments to pensioners must inevitably rise faster than the wage bill of contributing employees. In the past this has been disguised by inflation, so that contributions inflows increase with rising wages, and increases in the scope of pension funds. In this section the factors that will limit such increases in the future are examined.

The first limit to the growth of net contributions is simply the slow growth and, since 1990, the decline in employment in the main industrialized countries. This is apparent in Table 5.1. Such economic recession is particularly damaging to pension fund finances because firms usually respond to reduced demand by some combination of early retirement and freezing the intake of new workers, if not actually laying off employees. This has the effect of reducing the pool of contributing employees, while increasing the outflow of pension payments. Of course, if such a recession is confined to one industry, and other industries are still expanding, then the effect is similar to the 'serial maturity' discussed in Chapter 5. But if the recession is generalized then reduced contribution inflows overall reduces the flow of funds into securities markets. This in turn cuts back the growth of asset prices so that returns are much more likely to fall below those calculated by pension fund actuaries as necessary to keep pension funds solvent. Worse still, if the recession coincides with slow growth and recession in the other countries whose stock markets depend on pension fund surpluses, then even international diversification will not keep up returns to the funds' asset portfolios. As the employment growth figures show in Table 5.1, slow growth has characterized the three main economies, the UK, the US and Japan, whose capital markets have been most inflated by pension fund surpluses since the 1970s.

But even with a non-expanding work force, net contributions could still rise over time if there were sufficient wage inflation. This is because wage inflation increases the nominal value of contributions. Even if it also increases

Table 6.1 Inflation in industrialized economies (annual % change in consumer prices)

	1980–89	1990–95	1996
France	7.3	2.4	2.0
Germany	2.9	3.4	1.5
Italy	11.2	5.2	3.9
UK	7.4	4.4	2.4
EU* average	7.2	4.1	2.5
Japan	2.5	1.7	0.1
US	5.5	3.5	2.9
Advanced economies**	5.8	3.4	2.2

Source: National Westminster Bank Market Intelligence Department, *Economic and Financial Outlook*, February 1998.

Notes
* Fifteen member countries of the European Union.
** European Union plus the United States, Canada, Japan, Australia, New Zealand, Norway, Switzerland and Iceland.

future pension liabilities, where pensions are related to earnings in employment, the difference between the present pensions outflow and the contributions inflow will still rise in nominal or money terms, while current pension payments remain less than contributions. However, the rate of increase in wages over time tends to change with the more general rate of inflation. As Table 6.1 shows, the rate of consumer price increase in the industrialized countries has on the whole fallen since the 1980s.

By the 1990s, the main capitalist economies had put in place policy mechanisms for holding down inflation by deflationary monetary policies. These generally consist of requiring the central bank, whether independent or not, to offset increases in demand in the economy by raising interest rates. This has the effect of squeezing the expenditure of indebted households and firms, by raising the amount of their income which they must pay to service their debt.[1] In Europe the anti-inflationary regime inaugurated by the Maastricht Treaty provisions for European Monetary Union in 1993 also included requirements for reduced government deficits which has resulted in higher taxes and reduced government expenditure, especially on capital works which benefit the private sector. The squeeze on companies' liquidity because of high real interest rates and reduced fiscal deficits causes them to reduce expenditure on employment, materials and investment. Weak demand in the economy therefore discourages price rises. But this deflationary squeeze also dissuades companies from employing additional workers or replacing employees who retire or leave.

Reduced expenditure on employment results in a fall in pension fund contributions. In this situation, any corresponding fall in pension liabilities affects only future pension payments: current pension payments may rise if companies retire workers early even with reduced pensions. Thus the anti-inflationary fervour of the 1990s not only precludes a mechanism for stabilizing inflows into capital markets, but also maintains a state of incipient recession that chokes off those inflows.

Long-term investments in insurance and pension funds are characteristic of households enjoying secure and reasonably well-paid employment. The relatively high income elasticity of demand for pensions and insurance has also meant that, in an economic decline, pension and insurance investment declines more than proportionately. According to the Central Statistical Office's *Financial Statistics*, the net inflow of funds into pension funds and insurance companies in the UK fell from a peak of £37.2bn in 1990 to £28bn in 1994. It is difficult to disentangle from this trend the effects of the economic recession of the time, which might have given rise to a temporary increase in households' liquidity preference from the effects of a more long-term trend in the labour market discussed below which may be reducing the income elasticity of demand for pensions and insurance. This would suggest that an increase in pensions contributions, relative to any increase in income, is likely to be less in the next economic recovery than it was in the past: hence, the contributions and premium inflow into pension funds and insurance companies is unlikely to rise again as fast as it did in previous recoveries, while the outflow of pension payments will continue to rise.

Reduced net contribution inflows into pension funds would not affect the solvency of those funds if returns on their investments were maintained. As indicated in Chapter 5, those inflows now dominate the capital markets of the world. Reduced inflows would therefore be associated with lower returns unless the scope of funded pension schemes is extended to include workers currently not in funded schemes. A minor problem is that in the UK, the US and Japan, pension schemes are largely already funded, and the scope for taking in new workers is severely limited. In a world of free portfolio capital flows between financial centres, this limitation does not matter so much, because there are other countries where large groups of workers do not yet belong to funded schemes, or whose funded schemes are strictly regulated by the government. These countries are predominantly in Western Europe. By the mid-1990s, a campaign had been established in the media and among economists and politicians to discredit government-financed pension schemes, on the grounds that they involve an insupportable burden on the tax-payer.[2] Since the discussion here is concerned with the solvency and financial stability of funded pension systems we do not enter into that particular controversy. Suffice it to say that the battle to wean German and Italian workers from their state pensions is not just a struggle for sound government finance. Perhaps even more importantly, it is a struggle to save the soundness of the capital markets of the US, the UK and Japan and the solvency of their funded pension schemes. For, with failing inflows into pension schemes in those countries, new inflows are necessary to support their capital markets.

But even if Western Europeans, seized of the fiscal perils of state pensions, were to embrace funded pension schemes more widely, this could only be a temporary measure. As in the case of serial maturity, the scope of funded pensions would need to continue to be increased to avoid a situation in which the rate of growth of contributions inflows slows down to the rate of growth earnings and employment in the countries covered by the schemes, while pensions payments rise exponentially until the retired population stabilizes. The longer term problem is that there are few countries outside Western Europe, North America and Japan without funded pensions schemes but with a sufficiently large stratum of employees earning sufficiently high incomes to make up shortfalls in pension fund inflows in the wealthy industrialized countries. The industrialized and semi-industrialized countries of Eastern Europe, Latin America and East and South Asia have groups of highly paid employees, but these are relatively small. Thus the confined circle of stable, highly paid and pensionable employment provides a third limitation on the ability of funded pension schemes to maintain their inflows and support asset prices in the world's capital markets.

And even within the heartland of those capitalist countries devoted to the cult of finance, there is a fourth factor at work undermining the stability of funded pension schemes. This is the increasing extent of the casualization of labour. There is now a growing political consensus that the increasingly acute problem of unemployment apparent in most countries is due to the 'inflexibility' of the labour force, i.e., the stubborn preference of the unemployed for jobs that are stable and reasonably paid, and the seemingly mulish reluctance of the employed to let their conditions of pay and employment become subject to arbitrary variation by employers in line with business conditions. Such inflexibility is supposed to be supported by welfare state provisions that allow the unemployed to refuse jobs that are offered to them, however unstable and low-paid these might be. The theory behind this suggests that if employees accept variable rates of pay and hours of work, in line with the market situation of the employer, then employment, in the sense of the numbers in work, would become stable and employers would be more willing to employ more workers. In this way, it is argued, unemployment would be reduced. It is now widely supposed that this has been the way in which employment in the US has been increased since the mid-1980s (see Table 5.1). Britain has been foremost among European countries in adopting policies to make labour more 'flexible' and rising unemployment in Germany and Japan during the 1990s has been widely attributed to the alleged 'inflexibility' of their employment arrangements.

Whether there is indeed any connection between secure, remunerative employment and unemployment is outside the scope of this analysis. What is beyond dispute is that a declining proportion of the labour force in Japan, the US and the UK has stable, well-paid employment. In such circumstances, a worker facing uncertain prospects of employment and income is unlikely to find pension schemes, or any other kind of long-term savings, attractive or appropriate to her or his needs. Unemployment, or the threat of it, may persuade employees to be more accommodating of their employers' financial circumstances. But it is more difficult for households to tailor their consumption to the resulting fluctuations in their income. It is easier to maintain consumption if there are readily accessible savings on which to draw to make up any shortfall in income. A 'flexible' worker is therefore likely to have what Keynes called, in another context, a high 'liquidity preference'.[3] In other words, should his or her income be high enough to allow saving out of it, then such savings are best accumulated in a liquid form where they would be accessible in the event of unemployment or some other sudden drop in income. If there is some illiquid investment that would be appropriate, it is likely to be the purchase of the house or flat in which she or he lives, providing at least a secure home for the worker and her or his family. If the worker's income is not high enough to afford saving, then she or he will most likely seek to reduce deductions from that income by avoiding pensions contributions, or working in the cash economy to avoid all deductions: survival on a low income precludes worry about income in retirement as long as hope can be placed in the possibility of getting stable employment, or a win in the National Lottery. Should the worker find him or herself in secure, gainful employment in the years approaching retirement, then she or he might become susceptible to the tax advantages of funded pension schemes and compounded returns on them. But, with years to go before retirement, more immediate consumption is more pressing. In general, tying up savings in long-term pension funds is unsuitable for workers facing uncertainty about future income and employment. In this way, the casualization of labour reduces the willingness of workers to contribute to pension schemes, and diminishes the pool of the employed labour force from which contributions may be taken.[4]

This rise in liquidity preference is likely to affect not only households without any member in stable, reasonably paid employment. Households with one or even two members in good employment are still liable to increase their liquidity preference as long as they have members studying, or unemployed, or in insecure employment, and whose ability to pay for future consumption is thereby made uncertain. A positive benefit of a comprehensive and easily accessible welfare state is that by removing uncertainty about the affordability in the future of current living standards it facilitates long-term saving. The paradoxical aspect of such a welfare state is that long-term saving is no longer necessary to support consumption. In this way, comprehensive welfare changes the purpose of saving and finance from prudent assurance of current living standards to personal enrichment and the financial accumulation which was seen as its purpose in the years of classical political economy.

6.2 Capital market disintermediation

The end of funded pension schemes is inevitably a speculative matter that is best approached by rationally disposing of the most common preconceptions about it. The first of these preconceptions is that funded pension schemes, prudently and honestly managed, are proof against changes in the net inflow of funds into them; in particular that returns on their investments, conservatively compounded and projected into the future by the schemes' actuaries, can be maintained at the rates necessary to meet the schemes' pension liabilities. This might be the case, if their investments were being channelled through perfect capital markets in which the asset sales and purchases of the schemes did not affect returns on those investments. However, it is not the case in capital markets which have been inflated by pension fund surpluses to the point where pension funds or their agents own the majority of securities, and in markets where the transactions of the funds and their agents easily dominate the market. In such a situation, it is not possible for funds to reduce their net purchases of assets without causing a reduction in the growth of asset prices, and hence a reduction in returns to their investments.

A second view, that is somewhat less favoured, nevertheless worries some financiers and some regulatory institutions, although they will not admit it openly. According to this, when the funded pension schemes eventually reach maturity, i.e., when their pension payments will exceed the inflow of contributions and investment income, financial assets will have to be sold on such a scale as to cause securities markets to crash, and the pension funds to collapse into insolvency. This possibility is unlikely because it does not take into account two essential features of pension fund finance analysed above. The first is that, prior to maturity, the funds will go through a period of decline in net contributions inflows, during which any excessive pension liabilities may be met from investment income. As a result of this decline in contributions, the funds' reduced buying of assets will reduce the liquidity of capital markets and decrease the returns on those assets. If this decrease reaches the point when additional contributions have to be made, either by employers or by employees, or benefits have to be reduced, questions will inevitably be asked about the management of the funds. Their managers' unblemished records of probity and caution will be useless if the financial flows resulting from the *aggregate* activity of the funds cause returns on investments to fall below even conservative actuarial calculations.

The second element of the analysis which will become a factor in the decline of pension funds even before maturity is the distribution of their assets between locally integrated and peripheral markets. As returns to fund investments are reduced, with the fall in net contributions inflows, peripheral markets will become more attractive. Fund managers who invest in a small market and are followed by other fund managers will record superior returns to the funds under their management. This will encourage pension funds to entrust more of their portfolios to their care. However, unless they can persuade other managers to follow them again, and with more funds in proportion to the increased funds entrusted to them, then it is likely that some other markets and some other manager will subsequently record superior returns. In this way pension fund money will be drawn to more speculative investments and under the control of specialists in the manipulation of market sentiment.

Falling cash inflows into pension schemes also make their portfolios less malleable. A pension fund with a large cash inflow may change the proportion of its portfolio allocated to particular types of investment simply by concentrating its purchases on those securities whose share in the portfolio it wishes to increase. However, with a small or negligible inflow, changing the proportions in the portfolio is much more likely to require the sale of securities. Given the tendency of investment managers to invest and realize assets in a conventional way, sales of assets tend to be concentrated in particular markets, rather than widely dispersed. Among the consequences of maturing pension schemes is therefore much greater selling pressure in particular markets.

The decline of funded pension schemes will have serious and widespread consequences. The most catastrophic are likely to be for pensioners dependent on those schemes. Having contributed, together with their employers, to these schemes they will find the scheme's eventual inability to give the promised benefits incomprehensible and will inevitably blame the managers of them. This would be unfair to those managers since it is argued in these chapters that the fault lies in the financial structure of the funded pension system as a whole, rather than with the administrators of any particular scheme. However, as noted above, with reduced returns in integrated markets, enough money may have been entrusted to fund managers specializing in market manipulation to discredit many more honest managers and financiers.

Another reaction to reduced returns may be for funded pensions schemes to reduce benefits. This is already happening in the US and Britain, with new funds tending to opt for Defined Contribution or Money Purchase schemes, in which the eventual pension merely reflects the payments into the scheme and actual returns on the payments invested, rather than Defined Benefits schemes, in which the benefits are guaranteed. Defined Contribution schemes are merely a more complex with-profits life assurance policy. Like these policies, they are attractive when the capital market is being inflated and investment returns are good. However, when they are merely a way to pass on poorer investment returns to pensioners, such returns will be an additional incentive to workers to opt out of complex and illiquid saving schemes and stick to readily accessible savings.

The effect of declining pension fund surpluses on securities markets will be to make 'integrated' markets more peripheral, and peripheral markets less stable. With reduced inflows, pension funds will have less liquidity available to use to support markets, even if prolonged and heavy selling in them seriously threatens the value of the most secure 'blue chip' assets in their portfolios. Indeed, with growing pension commitments, the funds will need to keep more of their assets liquid. To maintain this liquidity, purchases of equities and long-term stocks will need to fall faster than the decline in net inflows. In this situation, 'integrated' markets in the US, the UK and Japan will become less liquid, and securities market crashes will be more difficult to overcome. With increasing illiquidity in securities markets, the onset of maturity will threaten the solvency of pension funds which have not prepared themselves for this eventuality either by holding more assets in a more liquid short-term form (as Treasury or company bills for example) or in bonds maturing as pension funds themselves mature. But a shift on any significant scale in portfolio distribution, from equity towards bonds, would induce exactly that illiquidity in equity markets whose avoidance would be intended by such a precautionary shift. Thus Ponzi finance structures have a way of committing to their survival everyone implicated in them.

For governments and companies, the decline of funded pension schemes will be an inconvenience rather than a disaster. Companies which have financed themselves through the issue of shares or common stock will find that the price of their stock will fail to rise as expected and they are more likely to have difficulty in issuing new shares. Their senior managers may well be disappointed by the cessation of past gains from stock options, secured as pension funds inflated the market.[5]

In the US some companies, like Citicorp, already have major programmes for buying in their stock, although more securely with their own reserves rather than borrowed money. This is one of the reasons why the US stock market has kept booming through the 1990s. But the tactic of companies buying back their own shares in this way raises fundamental questions which go to the heart of the analysis in this book. Securities markets are supposed to raise finance for companies. The use of companies' finance to support the market in this way, rather than investing in equipment and technology, implies an economic system in which enterprises raise finance for the capital markets, rather than the other way around. Arguably, buying in stock by companies can only have a limited and temporary effect. The stocks of companies with a lot of liquid reserves could benefit. Stocks of companies with less reserves, or which are not targeted for takeover by companies with more reserves, may not be affected. It is also questionable whether companies could mobilize such volumes of saving as pension funds were able to. In this way, the market in which 'efficient' trade takes place would contract to a much smaller range of stocks of companies that happen to be quite liquid. These would inevitably be the less investment-intensive companies and would further discourage manufacturing and heavy industry.

In a less liquid capital market, companies and governments have difficulty in 'rolling over' stock, i.e., issuing new bonds to repay old ones. In this situation, they will inevitably turn to the banking system for new finance. The return of their best customers should revive the fortunes of banks, except perhaps those which have committed themselves most heavily to securities trading and fund management.

Perhaps the most important effect of less buoyant capital markets will be the demystification of capital gains in those markets. This should assist in promoting more rational attitudes towards finance and a more critical view of the use of welfare provision to support capital market inflation. The capital market may provide effective liquidity when it is a facility for the corporate treasurer whose operations are modest and discreet. With inflation, the apparent growth in market liquidity is all too precarious, if only because of the rapid rise in claims on that liquidity.

Thus, as maturity approaches, capital markets become more fragile and less liquid. The disappointment of expectations, and the failure of fund management ventures, will suggest that those expectations were exaggerated and fraudulently exploited. More careful examination of the process and effects of capital market inflation reveals that exaggerated expectations are justified at the beginning of such a process, and thwarted towards the end of it, by the objective structures of financial liabilities created by financial inflows into the capital markets, and changes in those financial inflows.

Part III
Financial derivatives and liquidity preference

7 Liquidity preference and the conventional approach to financial futures

He (John Law) told Pitt that he would bring down our East India stock, and entered into articles with him to sell at 12 months hence, a hundred thousand pounds of stock at eleven per cent under the present current price.[1]

Towards the end of August 1719, Thomas Pitt, Lord Londonderry, dined in Paris with John Law, who was shortly to be appointed Contrôlleur-Général des Finances, effectively Prime Minister, to the French King Louis XV. Law was then in the process of organizing the repayment of the French national debt by his Mississippi Company, and was consumed with a sense of his own financial genius. He seems to have believed that France, under his financial direction, was destined to push Britain into the margins of finance and trade, causing investors to abandon British securities for shares in his Mississippi Company, the market for which was being inflated using credit money created by Law's own Banque Royale.[2] A contract with Lord Londonderry was drawn up and signed on 29 September 1719. Under this contract, His Lordship was to pay Law £180,000 in exchange for £100,000 of shares in the East India Company, a year thence. At the end of September 1719, East India shares cost £192 per £100 of shares. By June 1720 their price had risen to £420 at which price Law's prospective loss on the contract was £240,000. Law made various margin payments on the contract but, in the months that followed, the Mississippi Company collapsed, and in December 1720, Law fled France. It is unlikely that he ever fully settled his contract with Lord Londonderry.[3]

Law's contract was what would today be called a forward contract, i.e., a future financial commitment whose terms are agreed when it is entered into, rather than the standardized futures contract traded in futures markets. That agreement was the prototype of today's futures contracts.

7.1 Financial futures in context

Financial futures may be regarded as a particularly neo-classical answer to what Keynes regarded as his quintessential contribution to political economy, his theory of liquidity preference. According to his theory, uncertainty causes economic agents in general, and rentiers in particular, to prefer to hold liquid assets rather than engage in long-term investment. This is supposed to prevent the capital market from functioning properly because rentiers demand higher interest rates on their long-term financial assets to compensate them for the possibly lower liquidity of those assets. These higher interest rates then discourage entrepreneurs from investing in all but the more profitable ventures.[4] Thus, financial futures appear as a spontaneous and ardently competitive set of markets projecting a web of certain prices into an uncertain future, banishing the uncertainty that is the black hole in inter-temporal general equilibrium and the cause of Keynesian pessimism about free market capitalism.

However, the limitations of existing financial futures markets in this regard seem fairly obvious. These include the short-term nature of their contracts and the narrow range of predominantly financial parameters which may be secured through them. In terms of effecting an inter-temporal general equilibrium, financial futures markets are deficient because they deal in nominal values, rather than relative prices. Less obvious are the nature of the competition in those markets, the actual operations of the agents in those markets, the resulting market mechanisms, the effects of these on liquidity in the economy, and the role of all these factors in capital market inflation.

Part III of this book provides a critical account of financial futures markets placing them in the context of finance-led contemporary capitalism. This chapter argues that the orthodox approaches to the analysis and regulation of financial derivatives are ambiguous and contradictory, in seeing such instruments as reducing financial risk, and simultaneously as sources of additional financial risk. The mainstream approach, in the Black-Scholes and most capital asset pricing models, is shown to use conceptually flawed methods of valuation that have only a tenuous foundation in reality.

The neo-classical analysis of financial futures instruments, based on perfect competition among profit-maximizing investors turns out to be inconsistent with the rationale for financial futures markets in that analysis as projecting certain values into an uncertain future. This kind of analysis does not take into account the weak competitive structure of financial futures markets, and the emergence in recent years of three classes of agent operating in financial futures markets, namely industrial and commercial companies, banks or brokers, and investment funds, each with their own distinctive interests, modes of operation in derivatives markets and criteria of success in using derivatives instruments. Their emergence, as well as financial instability and large capital inflows into financial markets, account for the rapid expansion of financial futures markets in recent years. An analysis of how they value their financial futures instruments is presented in Chapters 8 and 9, based on this distinction between these three classes of agent and the degree of monopoly of brokers in markets for differentiated derivatives instruments. In Chapter 10 the principles of regulating derivatives trading are discussed, with a critique of the Basle Accord system of over-capitalizing against gross outstanding liabilities or total value at risk.

Finally in Chapter 10, the financial fragility associated with derivatives markets is examined. Financial futures markets do not depend on inflows of funds in the same way that markets for longer-term securities do. Nevertheless, the approaching maturity of investment funds which are the dominant investors in securities markets is likely to cause a shift in fund managers' portfolio preferences towards more speculative investment in riskier markets such as financial derivatives. Because investment funds are more prone to finance or hedge their financial futures with claims on other financial markets, an increase in those funds' investment in financial futures will cause more general instability in financial markets in the future, while industrial and commercial companies investing in financial futures are more likely to suffer unexpected drains on their liquidity due to this instability. The resulting increase in their uncertainty and hence their enhanced liquidity preference, would reduce correspondingly their willingness to engage in long-term investment in fixed capital and new technology.

Insofar as neo-classical theorists consider financial futures as part of a more general economic analysis, they tend to view these instruments as part of a perfectly intermediated world, thereby approaching more closely that inter-temporal general equilibrium in which social welfare is maximized.[5] In this, Part III, of the book a more complex view is presented, focusing on market mechanisms which may leave participants with large gains or losses whose amount may not be predictable. One interpretation of Keynesian uncertainty is that, in a non-ergodic or continually changing world, financial parameters are the link between a certain present and an unknown future. Financial parameters are therefore held to affect in particular entrepreneurial investment in fixed capital and the spot (i.e., for immediate delivery) markets for bonds and money.[6] The chapters in Part III use a somewhat narrower view of uncertainty, associating it with the unpredictability of the consensus on the value of financial parameters that market traders will arrive at on a particular day in the future. Participants in financial futures markets enter into contracts in order to profit from the consensus that eventually arrives. The liquidation of the resulting structure of short-term financial claims and liabilities results in financial flows that are potentially more destabilizing than the volatility of the underlying financial variables.

7.2 Some concepts in the theory of financial futures

The neo-classical view of financial futures markets is that they are a facility which project certain values into an uncertain future, or at least replace uncertain values with a 'certainty-equivalent value' that reflects future 'risks'. If this were the case then, other things being equal, one would expect a reduction in the liquidity preference due to uncertainty as the use of financial futures has proliferated since the 1970s. But other things have not been equal since the 1970s. There has been a greater holding of liquid assets by companies associated with larger capital market liabilities as well as increased volatility of financial parameters, all of which may have contributed to increased resort to financial futures.

But a general point may be made here, and argued in greater detail in Chapters 8 and 9, that the uncertainty associated with financial futures depends on the use to which a financial future is put: if the purpose of using financial futures is to fix financial parameters, then this would indeed reduce uncertainty and may reduce liquidity preference (other things being equal!); however, if the purpose of using financial futures is to obtain a profit, then these instruments may actually increase uncertainty. In the first case an uncertain parameter is fixed enabling a profit from some underlying activity to be calculated with less uncertainty. But in the second case the profit depends on the difference between the fixed financial parameter and its uncertain value in the future. Such differences are likely to be even more volatile than the parameter itself. In other words, where financial futures are used for investment, the profit is not made more certain, but may be less so. The Basle Accord's regulations imposing capital requirements on banks' financial futures liabilities (a form of compulsory liquidity preference) is an implicit recognition that financial futures do not create greater certainty.[7]

The conventional textbook analysis of financial futures, based on time series analysis of price data, holds that the values of financial futures instruments are determined by the fundamental values of the underlying assets, so that the rationale for financial futures exists because there are market imperfections. For example, exchange rates deviate from 'equilibrium' rates, stock prices deviate from 'fundamental' values, price differences have not been arbitraged away, or private information has not yet become public information (i.e., the markets are not strongly efficient). Neo-classical (market efficiency) theorists view financial markets as consensus-creating systems of information exchange. In the neo-classical system, the consensus emerges around fundamental capital asset values. By contrast, Keynes, in his beauty contest analogy of capital markets in which participants rate stocks according to how they think *average opinion* will rate them, regarded that consensus as purely conventional.[8]

Theories about financial markets in general, and financial futures in particular, describe how markets operate and determine prices. A good price theory should explain how markets operate in order to bring about the prices described by the theory. But even the most abstractedly mathematical price models make implicit assumptions about the market mechanisms which bring about the prices postulated in those models. Such models are commonly empirically validated by price equations of the form:

$$P_t = P^*_t + \varepsilon_t \qquad\qquad (7.1)$$

That is, the conventional neo-classical theories measure the deviations, ε_t, of actual prices, P_t, from fundamental values, P^*_t, and filter out those components of ε_t which coincide with 'significant' events such as announcements of company results, trade and inflation statistics.

At its most systematic, the neo-classical theory presupposes that a competitive equilibrium will determine fundamental values (P^*_t). Futures decisions are then dependant on a presumption that the state of perfect market equilibrium (proxied by average prices in the capital asset pricing models used to determine P^*_t) will be approached in historical time. Given a fixed volatility in the price of the underlying asset,[9] no income on that asset, constant short-term interest rates, perfectly elastic supply of credit at given rates of interest, a tax regime that is neutral in respect of trades, and zero transaction costs, relatively simple mathematical formulas can be derived to show the value of an options or, more generally, a futures contract.[10] Broadly, it is then worthwhile entering into a financial futures agreement providing that its price or premium, f_t, is below the deviation of the actual price from the perceived fundamental value, i.e., buy if:

$$f_t < (P_t - P^*_t)$$
or $\quad ft < \varepsilon t \qquad\qquad\qquad (7.2)$

or sell if:

$$f_t > (P_t - P)$$
or $\quad ft > \varepsilon_t \qquad\qquad\qquad (7.2')$

where ε_t represents the current deviation from fundamental value.[11]

Future deviations from fundamental values are allowed for in Black-Scholes and Cox-Ross methods of futures pricing by averaging recent deviations. The residual from average prices, and the variance of that residual, is treated as a probabilistic measure of the risk that the average price (presumed to be the fundamental value) will not be realized by the maturity date of the futures contract. There is an implicit assumption that, at the maturity date of the contract, the most probable price of the underlying security will be some *average* of past prices. In line with modern portfolio theory this is treated as a proxy for the fundamental value of that security.[12] Other possible values of that price are distributed around that mean in a normal distribution completely described by that mean and the standard deviation from it. Accordingly, the frequency of 95 per cent of possible maturity values is supposed to be encompassed within 2.46 standard deviations of that mean.

But the future is never like the present, or the past. Because economies and markets change over time, each day in those markets has its unprecedented developments, so that the past is not a *complete* guide to the future. Indeed, speculation would be impossible if the past could provide such directions about the future, while financial innovation may be regarded as an optimistic attempt to distinguish the future from the past. There is a degree of uncertainty (lack of knowledge) about the future which cannot be proxied by deviations from historical averages. In the equations above, ε_{t+n} (the deviation on the maturity of a futures contract) may not be in any stable relationship with the array of past ε. The absence of any such stable relationship is all the more likely when capital markets are irregularly inflated by the kind of financial inflows described in Chapter 5.

To the degree that there is some trend at work, evolution can be approximated by weighting the recent past more than the distant past. But there remains a fundamental limitation of probability calculations based on statistical inference for serious academic research and financial market practice. Here it is necessary to distinguish between, say, a lottery, a routinely repeated action which gives rise to different outcomes of a particular frequency distribution, and events in markets which are not routinely repeated. Market events occur not because they are probable, but because their antecedents and circumstances cause them to happen. An event that occurs with a perceived probability of less than 1 per cent is much more real than all the possible outcomes with higher probabilities that did not happen. It can only be seriously explained or anticipated by examining how it happened and why. Probability cannot explain in this logical sense. In a market, price determination is a series of events that are decided by the financial inflow into that market, rather than a lottery,[13] even if subsequently price statistics may be drawn up as frequency distributions. As financial markets become more volatile, probability becomes a less and less adequate guide to analysis. A fundamental methodological contradiction arises between the growing volatility of financial markets, which is the rationale for the existence of financial futures, and the widely used models for analysing and pricing financial futures based on the relative stability of financial markets. This volatility brings financial research into the domain of business cycle theory, rather than probability analysis. The integration of financial markets in a comprehensive theory of the business cycle is beyond the scope of this study. However, in Chapters 8 and 9 certain conceptual distinctions, which may be useful in such an extended analysis, are put forward and Chapter 8 considers a view of the financial derivatives markets as a 'peripheral' market affected disproportionately by changes in net inflows into capital markets.

Nevertheless, the neo-classical pricing theories have a certain practical significance in that the higher is the proportion of traders following these pricing methods the more likely they are to give the correct valuation, in the sense of anticipating a consensus view. In a comment on the practical significance of the Black-Scholes method of valuing options, the Chairman of the Chicago Board Options Exchange, William Floresh, described that significance as 'staggering' because 'without a mathematical model that could predict comfortably where options prices could fall, we would not have had the participation of big investors that we have seen'.[14] In other words, the value of Black-Scholes is not that it gives 'correct' answers, but that it gives answers which enable investors to use options markets on a larger scale.

Students wishing to learn about strategies investment in financial futures markets are commonly taught valuation formulae as the vehicles for understanding values in those markets. Even recently fashionable models which deviate from the assumptions of perfectly competitive equilibrium, such as theories of bubbles, 'information cascades' and 'chaos' postulate equilibrium values which are the reference point for somewhat longer and more extreme deviations.[15] However, such values cannot be independent of the way in which those markets operate. There are other trading strategies that are just as practical as using mathematical models for valuing futures instruments and which may be even more rational in the sense of being based on some understanding of what is happening in the markets. Traders may, for example, disaggregate recent deviations into those systematically associated with particular events and developments, and then anticipate how these will evolve in the future and what the resulting deviations will be. This is not necessarily what is commonly called a 'fundamentalist' strategy, because that usually means an assumption that deviations from fundamental values will eliminate themselves (i.e., that ε tends to zero). A more realistic view simply supposes that deviations will continue to occur, but that they will be deviations from past values, rather than some underlying equilibrium. This already happens in, for example, the foreign exchange market, where traders continually anticipate, often in a relatively ill-informed way, the consequences for their market of a continuous stream of official and unofficial statistical announcements ('statsbabble').[16]

A more subjective, but still rational, strategy that is highly appropriate to open-outcry financial futures markets is Keynes's 'beauty contest' approach, anticipating the future valuations of other traders and how these may differ from current valuations of P_t and f_t. In this approach, fundamental values, and therefore deviations from them, are not even considered. Trading strategy is here determined by psychological analysis of other traders' sentiments, wishes and desires. A third strategy may be to analyse the liquidity position and liabilities of traders and their claims against each other to determine where the most profitable 'forced' sales of assets, or their future purchases, will occur.

These 'alternative' strategies are all more realistic, in that they are based on induction from observed events and behaviour than the mathematical models based on deductions from unrealistic assumptions of perfectly competitive equilibrium. But for practical purposes, their greater realism has to be set against the disadvantage of the lengthy, serious analysis that they require before the value of a trading decision becomes apparent. This limits their usefulness to long-term, more considered investment than the rapid-fire deals in the open-outcry trading that prevails in the main financial futures markets. In those markets, the neo-classical Black-Scholes and Cox-Ross methods are superior: with computers to make the calculations, they provide virtually instantly programmable trading decisions. An individual trader may make many more trades during a trading day, making up in volume for the smaller profit margins that he or she may expect to obtain on the most commonly traded contracts. The computer-programmable, neo-classical valuation models are therefore an important factor in facilitating fuller utilization of trading capacity through the proliferation of inter-broker dealing.[17]

There is also an institutional inconsistency in the neo-classical pricing analysis, which becomes very important when conclusions are drawn from it for the regulation of financial futures trading. The analysis supposes that financial futures instruments are bought for profit, so that any losses are the result of an inadequate analysis of risk (i.e., an incorrect specification of ε) or an incorrect trading strategy, and large profits (and by implication large losses) are supposed to be eliminated by arbitrage in near perfectly competitive markets. In this way, that element of the analysis with the weakest ontological foundation, namely fundamental values, proxied in empirical analysis and practical pricing application by some average of past prices, is absolved of any blame when the market equilibrium fails to arrive. This happens, for example, when pricing strategies go wrong, when traders such as Barings' Nick Leeson try to corner a market, or when serious losses accrue. Such events suggest that trading in markets occurs out of equilibrium, that there is no perfectly competitive, or any other, equilibrium 'out there' in the markets, other than the accounting balance between purchase and sale, and that the equilibria or fundamental values used in finance theory are a useful and calculated, but no less arbitrary, fiction.

In the remaining chapters of this part a notion of value is developed that relies more on market convention. This view shows how the circumstances of different types of agent, and their use of financial instruments, affect their valuation of such instruments.

8 Commercial and investment uses of financial futures

8.1 Derivatives use by industrial and commercial firms

In the orthodox, neo-classical theory, the agents in futures markets are all investors, i.e., individuals and firms possessing wealth and seeking a return on that wealth, either in capital gain or in income through buying and selling assets in financial markets. Financial futures are treated as merely a form of financial asset on which a profit may be made. Industrial and commercial users of financial futures instruments are assumed to be either acting as investors or merely servicing in an undefined way their commercial activities without affecting what is happening in the financial markets. But a clear and widely accepted rationale for financial futures is not to profit from these contracts, but to avoid losses from activities in the real economy, in industry and commerce.

For industrial and commercial firms (entrepreneurs for short), financial futures are a form of insurance against adverse movements in financial parameters (such as interest rates and exchange rates) which affect their business. If financial futures can project certainty into an uncertain future, then the scope for their application is truly enormous, and covers virtually all economic activity in virtually all economies. If markets for financial futures are as close to perfect competition as we are often assured, then the use of these instruments should indeed be widespread. However, among non-financial firms they are used by only a handful of large companies, and market literature, while paying lip-service to the future 'risks' which may be avoided by using financial derivatives, emphasizes the profitable applications of financial futures, and the large losses which they may cause. Financial investment for such hazardous profits requires a long pocket to be able to sustain losses, and the large capital that needs to be tied up in supporting operations in these markets is clearly a deterrent to the widespread use of financial futures.

The reason why only a small number of large companies use financial futures to avoid risks is because such instruments are inferior to the much more commonly used liquidity preference as a means of avoiding financial risks. They are inferior because liquidity preference, in the sense of holding a hoard of liquid assets from which occasional cash flow deficits may be met (what Keynes called the 'precautionary motive' for liquidity), brings a positive and certain return in the form of interest on bank deposits, or some equivalent profit on liquid savings, such as holdings of short-term company paper. Financial futures are also inferior because liquidity preference is more versatile: liquid assets may be used to meet cash deficits arising from a very wide range of circumstances, whereas financial derivatives, like insurance policies, specify very particular losses which may be covered. Indeed, with financial innovation, financial futures become more complex and new contracts become available for fixing the values of less commonly used financial parameters. By narrowing the scope of the possible losses covered, such financial innovation makes the resulting contracts even more inferior to liquidity which has the capacity to insure all losses.

This dual function of financial futures, as a source of profit and as an insurance, has been pointed out elsewhere.[1] It gives rise to a contradiction over the socially optimal pricing of these instruments. If, on the one hand, they are sources of profit, then it is in the regulatory interest for the price to be high enough to discourage reckless trading. This is implicitly recognized in the Basle Accord, which originally required banks to set aside capital against the total value of their futures contracts, effectively raising the price of those contracts by the cost of the additional capital which has to be set against them. If, on the other hand, financial futures are an insurance against losses due to changes in financial parameters, then it is in the social interest that financial futures prices should be as low as possible, with minimal margin requirements, in order to spread their benefits among the largest number of users. Neo-classical market theorists would argue that there is no contradiction here since the prices at all times should cover the risk entailed. However, equilibrium pricing according to current market supply and demand may not give the same result as actuarial calculations of possible future loss. Hence the regulatory issue of how to set margins and capital adequacy requirements remains open to dispute.

In this book three distinct classes of agents in financial markets have been postulated. Each of them has its own distinctive interests and, together with the financial market authorities, these classes form a complete description of the agents in those markets. These agents are entrepreneurs (industrial and commercial companies), who use financial futures to avoid losses; rentiers (nowadays financial investment institutions), who use financial futures to obtain profits, and banks or brokers, who act as intermediaries and issue financial futures contracts. The existence of these three distinct classes of agents has been in practice concealed by two aspects of the way in which financial markets in developed capitalist economies have evolved. The first is the entry of large industrial and commercial companies to join specialist financial investment managers trading in financial markets. This is due to companies' own liquidity preference, which has enabled them to accumulate large stocks of liquid financial assets. That liquidity preference has been enhanced by the companies' over-capitalization, which requires them to hold large amounts of liquid reserves against their larger obligations to the capital markets.[2] Industrial and commercial companies' treasury divisions now effectively operate as separate cost and profit centres within these large companies. At the peak of the boom in Tokyo's financial markets at the end of the 1980s, many large Japanese companies were reported to be making more profit from their treasury activities than from their traditional commercial, manufacturing and exporting business.

The second aspect of financial markets which has tended to conceal the distinctive operations of industrial and commercial companies is the relatively recent emergence of modern financial futures in the era of financial instability, following the breakdown of the Bretton Woods system of fixed exchange rates and the widespread abandonment of Keynesian monetary policy aimed at holding interest rates low. This instability has affected financial parameters as well as financial flows. Financial futures markets are supposed to offer ways of avoiding such instability, commonly not by fixing the parameters, but by guaranteeing to pay the difference between the contract or strike price and the actual price. Such instability is held to affect virtually all companies, but in actual fact most of its consequences are purely notional, or valuational (see Chapter 2). Except where a change in an exchange rate or interest rate has a significant effect on actual cash flows, changes in such financial parameters should not affect an industrial or commercial company's income and expenditure. To the chagrin of the purveyors of financial futures contracts, most industrial and commercial companies do not make any use of financial futures. As noted above, they use more practical and less costly ways of managing their cash flow (e.g., increasing their liquidity preference by holding large precautionary deposits, engaging in leads and lags for foreign exchange conversion, and borrowing or issuing securities at fixed interest rates). The main users of financial futures instruments remain banks and brokers.

Notwithstanding the recent dabbling of large corporations in financial speculation, the characteristic activity of entrepreneurs is making profits from production and trade, rather than operations in financial markets. Insofar as they use financial markets, it is to transfer payments, to borrow and to raise capital to finance and refinance their trade and production activities. These financial operations are subsidiary to and in principle should be designed to accommodate the main purpose of entrepreneurs' activity, which is to secure a return on their capital in the form of profits on the production, exchange and transport and distribution of goods and non-financial services. When acting as entrepreneurs rather than rentiers, industrial and commercial companies may use financial futures instruments to avoid anticipated losses on these non-financial activities. Hence, entrepreneurs tend to use exchange rate futures, interest rate agreements and currency swaps, rather than more strictly financial derivatives instruments like stock index futures, in order to protect their cash flow from adverse changes in exchange rates, interest rates and commodity prices.

Let us call the financial parameter whose adverse movement is being anticipated P_e. The entrepreneur will consider a financial futures contract in P_e at time t if he fears that the parameter's future value, $P_{e,t+n}$, will be greater than his preferred future value, $P^*_{e,t}$, in the case of a cost or cash outflow, or $P_{e,t+n}$ will be less than $P^*_{e,t}$, in the case of a revenue or cash inflow, at time t+n when the inflow or outflow is due. This price difference, multiplied by some scalar, q, of the company's operations that are affected by the financial parameter shows the loss which the company is anticipating. For a cost, or cash outflow, this anticipated loss, $L^*_{c,t}$ is therefore given by the expression:

$$(P^*_{e,t} - P_{e,t+n})q_{c,t+n} = L^*_{c,t} \qquad (8.1)$$

For a revenue or cash inflow, this anticipated loss is:

$$(P_{e,t+n} - P^*_{e,t})q_{r,t+n} = L^*_{r,t} \qquad (8.1')$$

In the case of a parameter affecting costs and revenues, this expected loss is the sum of the above expressions:

$$(P_{e,t+n} - P^*_{e,t})q_{r,t+n} + (P^*_{e,t} - P_{e,t+n})q_{c,t+n} = L^*_t \qquad (8.1'')^3$$

In a world in which expectations are frequently and irregularly confounded, it is also possible that the financial parameter in question may actually move in a favourable way for the company, i.e., $P_{e,t+n}$ may be greater than $P^*_{e,t}$, in the case of a revenue or cash inflow, or it may be less in the case of a cost or cash outflow. If this is expected, then clearly the company will not consider using financial futures contracts or will use an option, because it will profit from the movement of the financial parameter. If this favourable movement is not expected, then the company will have committed itself to a financial agreement which is less favourable than the benefit from not having entered into the agreement at all. But this loss is notional rather than actual: it is reasonable to suppose that the financial parameter being fixed by the futures contract is set at a level that gives an expected profit to the company from the commercial transaction represented by the scalar q. As a result of fixing that parameter, the expected profit is realized or, at least, any shortfall is not due to the contract entered into but is due to the company's uncovered operations. These may have been uncovered because the markets do not have contracts for such contingencies (e.g., competitive pressures, business cycle fluctuations) or because the company preferred to make its own internal arrangements for coping with the contingency, or because the price at which the contract is offered is above what the company is willing to pay for it, so that the company is induced by the futures price offered in the market to make its own internal arrangements for accommodating the loss.

This leads on to the question of how much the company will be prepared to pay for a financial futures contract guaranteeing it a price of $P^*_{e,t}$ at time t+n. In principle, L^*_t should be the upper bound on the fee or premium that the company will be prepared to pay in order to eliminate the loss that it expects to make as a result of the expected shift in financial parameter P to $P_{e,t+n}$. It would be irrational for the company to pay in excess of L^*_t for the contract, since it would then be paying more to eliminate the anticipated loss than it expects the loss to be. Its willingness to pay any price below L^*_t depends on the size of the projected loss, relative to its total profit – a small enough loss may be deemed negligible and not worth the transaction costs of the contract. Furthermore, there are alternative ways of eliminating or reducing the expected loss: in the case of the foreign exchange example given below, these would be leads and lags, foreign currency deposits and matching transactions. The last of these is a tactic that is particularly relevant to the analysis in this book: using a foreign currency cash inflow to pay bills in the same foreign currency is, in form at least, Minsky's least risky form of financing, hedge finance. Obviously the lower is the price of the financial futures contract, the more likely the company is to consider it preferable to these alternative methods. In brief, the entrepreneur's willingness to use financial futures is in proportion to the relative size of his exposure to fluctuating financial parameters, and in negative proportion to the price of a financial futures contract that would protect them against a loss due to such fluctuations, relative to the size of that loss.

Three other remarks may be made about the financial futures contracts to eliminate entrepreneurs' expected losses from variations in financial parameters. First of all, only realized expected losses appear in the accounts of a company. The actual profits or losses entered into the income and expenditure accounts of the entrepreneurial company arise out of the commercial and industrial activity of the company, whereas the expected losses considered here are the revenues lost (or the additions to costs) due to anticipated changes in the financial parameters to which the company's activities are exposed, including expected changes that never occurred. Expected losses are notional, or contingent losses which depend on the entrepreneur's subjective evaluation of future changes in financial parameters. Because of uncertainty about those changes and their industry-specific nature, the realism of these evaluations cannot be programmed by computer or decided by outside financial advisers, although they may be informed by them. They depend principally on the situation of the company in its markets, and on the experience of its managers.

Second, commercial and industrial companies, as such, do not enter into matching financial futures contracts, in the sense of exactly equal and opposite contracts. In other words they do not hedge their futures contracts in the financial futures market. The interest of these companies is in stabilizing the cash flow generated by their non-financial business, rather than in generating additional cash flow. Moreover, if contracts are exactly matched, then the gain on one would equal the loss on the other, and the company would have to pay in addition the two fees or commissions that would be the price of the contracts.

Third, there is in practice not just one preferred financial parameter, P, or its expected level in the future. There will be a whole range of possible values of P, which the company can array in its order of preference. There will also be a range of future values of P, which the market will order according to the fee for a standard contract (see Chapter 9). In general, when industrial and commercial companies use financial futures contracts to secure more preferred values of P, they enter into contracts to pay fees that are less than their expected loss. If companies had known and stable preference functions for particular values of P, and financial futures brokers had fixed and stable pricing policies, a market equilibrium could be determined, providing that there is some overlap between the prices that companies are prepared to pay for fixing preferred parameters and the prices that brokers require for those parameters. However, company preferences are determined by their commercial business and, like that, they evolve over time. By contrast, pricing policies in financial futures markets depend on the current conjuncture in financial markets, volatile expectations about it, the individual broker's need to hedge or match uncovered positions, as well as changes in the most commonly used futures pricing models.

The financial futures activity of industrial and commercial firms can be illustrated in the following example. Let us suppose that a company manufactures a particular product for export to Germany, where its sales are invoiced in Deutschmarks. All production costs are in the UK, but the company is clearly exposed to the risk that the Deutschmark will depreciate against the pound sterling. It may convert DM300m of sales proceeds in a year's time. Let us further suppose that the current rate of exchange of DM3 per UK£ would give the company sales proceeds of £100m, and the company finds this rate of exchange acceptable because it offers an adequate return on its capital. But the company expects the Deutschmark to depreciate to DM3.50 per UK£ in a year's time, which would give it sterling sales proceeds of £85.7m, and a notional loss of £14.3m, due to that depreciation. This notional loss of £14.3m therefore represents the limit on what the company is prepared to pay to avoid this loss by entering into a futures contract to convert DM300m into sterling in one year's time at a rate of DM3 per UK£.

Clearly the company will not pay more than this, since the contract would then cost more than the loss that it anticipates. Whether the company would be willing to pay £14m, or £1.4m, or any money at all, to fix the rate for the DM300m at DM3 per £ depends on the alternative methods available to the company for dealing with the projected loss: in this case it may be able to use leads and lags to avoid the depreciation by converting on a different date, simply holding the foreign currency for a longer period of time, i.e., increase its liquidity preference. The company's willingness to pay a particular price for fixing the exchange rate also depends on its attitude towards the projected loss of £14.3m. This depends not just on those deeply subjective factors that are the staple of risk and expectations analysis: its so-called 'risk-aversion'. It is also influenced by what is happening to other competitors (who may be even worse affected by the depreciation) and therefore reporting smaller losses than those competitors may actually be to the advantage of the company; by its fiscal position; and by the degree of (capital market) pressure for the company to maximize the return on its capital.

The projected loss of £14.3m will not appear in the company's statement of income and expenditure. Even if the company ends up converting its export sales proceeds at the depreciated rate, what will actually appear will be sales revenue of £85.7m, rather than the £14.3m lost because of the less favourable exchange rate. In this sense the losses due to changes in financial parameters are notional, because they are always relative to some more or less arbitrary (and hence, less or more realistic) preferred level in those parameters from which the loss is measured.

Finally, the company will not enter into matched contracts to sell and buy DM300m in the future, because the company's actual exposure to exchange rate fluctuations arises out of its commercial business, which leaves it with that amount of foreign currency to convert. If its commercial business was exactly matched, so that it had exactly DM300m of costs to set against revenue of this amount at the time of its receipt, the equation (8.1″) would show no projected loss, and the company would have no commercial or industrial need to enter into sterling-Deutschmark futures contracts.

8.2 Derivatives use by rentiers

There is a second class of agent operating in the financial futures markets with unmatched positions. These are investors, or rentiers as they may be called to distinguish them from industrial and commercial investors in fixed capital or material and manufactured stocks. Rentiers in the past were individuals who held their own portfolios of financial investments. Today, as indicated in Chapter 3, they are principally insurance companies and pension funds, and various investment managers managing financial assets on behalf of insurance and pension funds. The characteristic feature of rentiers is that they seek a return on their capital by trading in financial markets, and hence have, or control, assets in a range of financial markets. Thus the essential difference between entrepreneurial and rentier capital is the kind of operations from which they seek their return. The simplifying assumption that firms operate either as entrepreneurs, rentiers or the bankers/brokers described in the next chapter is maintained. In Chapter 10 some of the consequences of removing this assumption are considered.

The rentiers' mode of using financial futures instruments differs from that of entrepreneurs in another very fundamental way. Entrepreneurs use financial futures contracts to avoid the consequences of deviations from preferred values of financial parameters because entrepreneurs have little influence

over those parameters and deviations. By contrast, rentiers by and large
themselves determine those financial parameters but determine them as a
class. For rentiers, financial parameters are endogenous data. They fix them
by the daily creation and re-creation of a consensus among the leading
traders in the markets on the values of those parameters, through arbitrage,
reputation, tacit understandings, covert rumour, overt trading and the
exchange of information in the financial press.[4] Financial futures trading
therefore takes place in a semi-informed ignorance of what the eventual
consensus will be, as a way of profiting from that consensus as well as influencing it.

In financial futures trading, the rentier, or in practice his or her fund
manager, estimates the future value of a financial parameter by any rational
(or irrational) means. This is the $P^*_{ri,t+n}$. He or she next compares this with
the future values indicated by other traders in screen trading quotations, or
on the boards in board trading, or the calls in open-outcry trading, or the
financial press and information system. Let us suppose that these indicate
different expected values among them, say, a value $P^*_{rj,t+n}$ ($P^*_{ri,t+n} \neq
P^*_{rj,t+n}$). If in the process of finding out this market view on the future of
this financial parameter the rentier remains convinced of the initial estimate,
then a clear profit opportunity arises. The size of the expected profit depends
on the difference between this view from the market and the rentier's own
estimate, and the amount of money that the rentier is prepared to invest in
the contract (and the value of the contract that the counterparty holding the
view $P^*_{rj,t+n}$ is prepared to accept). This amount of invested money is a
scalar, $q_{p,r}$, applied to the price difference. It may be the full value of the
contract, if a deposit against the full amount of it is necessary when the
contract is agreed, or it may be a much larger amount, if only a margin
payment is required and the rentier intends to sell the contract before it
matures. The total expected profit, $\phi_{i,p,t}$, on the contract is therefore given by
the expression:

$$| P^*_{ri,t+n} - P^*_{rj,t+n} | .q_{p,r} / m = \phi_{i,p,t} \qquad (8.2)$$

where m is the margin that is being traded.

$\phi_{i,p,t}$ also sets the upper limit on the fee or premium that the rentier will be
prepared to pay for the contract. Deducting this fee, $F_{p^*,t}$ from the expected
profit gives the net profit on the contract, $\phi_{i,p,t} - F_{p^*,t}$. Therefore,

$$\frac{(\phi_{i,p,t} - F_{p^*,t})}{(P^*_{ri,t+n})/q_{p,r}/m}$$

represents the expected rate of return. Standardizing it for the amount of
time in which his or her capital ($P^*_{ri,t+n}.[q_{p,r}/m]$) will be tied up, the rentier
may compare a standardized expected rate of return with that on other
financial instruments available for investment by the rentier. In general then,

the lower is the fee (or the margin requirement), or the greater is the difference between the rentier's estimate of the future value of the financial and that of the market, the more profitable the contract will appear to be, and hence the greater will be the demand for it. But the more that the rentier's views on the future coincide with those of the emerging market consensus, the smaller is the expected profit likely to be because brokers offering the contract are more likely to demand a fee equivalent to that anticipated profit and their corresponding anticipated loss (unless they can profitably hedge their contract – see Chapter 9 below).

It should be noted that this expected profit is not an amount that is ever likely to find its way into the rentier's accounts, unless his or her expectations are fully realized. The value of the contract when it matures, or when it is sold, will reveal an actual profit or loss on the transaction that depends on conjunctural flows of funds between markets, and the market consensus on that conjuncture, which jointly determine the values of financial parameters in the spot and futures markets at any one time. Such is the caprice of financial market sentiment that this conjuncture and the market view on it may be, and frequently is, totally uncorrelated with the consensus at the time when the contract was entered into.

Unlike entrepreneurs who only need futures contracts to fix parameters or prices for financial inflows and outflows generated by their normal commercial business, rentiers who do not engage in industrial or commercial enterprise need to be able to secure an inflow of the underlying financial asset which a futures contract obliges them to deliver, or secure purchasers for deliveries made to them. Financial futures markets use one of three kinds of operation to settle such obligations on the maturity date of the contract. These may be met by transactions in the cash market, equivalent bank credit transfer or hedging in the futures market. Hedging in the cash market consists of buying or selling the financial instrument specified in the futures contract in the market for immediate delivery of the instrument, i.e., the foreign exchange market or the stock market. However, in the case of stock market index futures and interest rate futures, settlement usually consists of a bank credit transfer of the difference between the value of the financial instrument specified in the futures contract, and the instrument's value in the cash market ($\phi_{i,p,t}$ in equation 8.2). The third type of hedging is simply buying a matching futures contract which supplies the underlying asset to settle the obligation entered into under the original contract.

While all these operations enable rentiers to settle a financial futures contract, they do not ensure that it will be profitable. In the case of the first two settlement operations, profitability depends on the difference between the price specified in the contract and the price in the cash market. This is the gain or loss that the futures contract fee would have to cover if there were no possibility of hedging in the futures market. Hence in general, when fees are related to the expected gain or loss on a contract, the profit from speculating in such a contract is limited, or negligible.

However, if the fee is driven by competition below the expected gain or loss (see Chapter 9) then a substantial profit may be obtained, depending on movements in the cash market in the case of cash settlement, or on changes in the consensus in the futures market that enables a hedging contract to be bought, fixing a profit on the initial contract. Therefore, once a 'position is taken' in the futures market, and a futures contract is entered into, it is in the speculator's interest to influence the market consensus in the cash and the futures markets by publishing information and so-called 'disinformation', and even conspicuous trading. This kind of 'dirty' speculating makes a mockery of neo-classical notions that active financial markets disseminate information more efficiently.[5]

Financial futures markets are not only sensitive to developments in the spot market and financial flows in the economy as a whole. Fees in futures markets are also affected by the supply of and demand for particular contracts. Moreover, in today's markets investors need not hold any contract to maturity, but may sell and re-buy as often as they wish. Because of the relatively short maturity periods of financial futures instruments (three months is usual, and over six months is exceptional) rentiers' portfolios of futures contracts are much more changeable than portfolios of other financial instruments. Therefore at any one time there will be, in addition to new contracts demands from rentiers and entrepreneurs, a stock of outstanding contracts about to mature or available for re-sale. This makes supply and demand for particular contracts, and the resulting prices charged for them, very fluid and volatile.

As with entrepreneurs, a simple example illustrates the way in which rentiers operate in financial futures markets. Let us suppose that the rentier expects the Deutschmark to appreciate against the pound sterling in a year's time to DM2.50. However, for a certain fee, the rentier can get from the market a contract to buy Deutschmarks in a year's time at DM3 per UK£. Providing that the fee is less than 16.66' per cent of the contract value (i.e., the amount by which the rentier expects the Deutschmark to appreciate), it is profitable for the rentier to enter into contracts to buy Deutschmarks in a year's time at DM3 per UK£. To illustrate the point about the fluidity of futures portfolios, it may be noted that should the Deutschmark start to appreciate, and the market offer a contract to sell Deutschmarks at DM2.50 per UK£ for a sufficiently low fee, then it is possible for the rentier to secure the profit in advance, entering into that contract to sell at DM2.50 and thereby hedging his or her original contract.

Two aspects of this transaction should be noted. First of all, in order to profit from this transaction it has to be unmatched: the rentier will not enter into two contracts to buy and sell a given quantity of Deutschmarks (or any other financial asset) at the same rate, because the pre-fee profit on one transaction would exactly equal the loss on the other transaction. But by entering into an unmatched contract, the rentier creates an exposure to adverse changes in financial markets. If, instead of appreciating, the Deutschmark depreciated, the rentier would make a loss, and would certainly be unlikely to secure the profit by entering into the second 'hedging' contract to sell Deutschmarks for a sufficiently low fee. Even if the currency appreciated, a loss could still be made on the contract if the appreciation failed to cover the fee paid for the transaction. Hence, a lower fee reduces the potential loss. At zero fee, the only possible loss is if the currency depreciates. Notwithstanding the fee paid, the exposure due to unhedged futures commitments is the important element in the rentier's risk in investing in financial futures. Normally traders secure themselves against this risk by hedging their original exposure in the futures market, i.e., entering into an opposite contract at a different rate. However, their ability to guarantee their profit in this way depends upon a contract becoming available at a favourable rate and at a sufficiently low fee.

Furthermore, where the contract is covered by a transaction in the 'spot' market (in this case, if Deutschmarks bought when the futures contract matures are sold in the cash market) then this may cause difficulty in the cash market. So, for example, derivatives trading inspired the large-scale selling of stock that caused the 1987 stock market crash.[6]

The other noteworthy aspect of the transaction is the view of the counterparty, since the profit of the rentier (excluding the fee) is the loss of the counterparty issuing the contract. If the counterparty has the same information and expectations as the rentier then, to cover him or herself against that loss, the counter-party should charge a fee or premium that is at least as large as the profit that the rentier is (commonly) expected to make. But if the counterparty does this, then the rentier will not enter into that contract because it would earn no profit after the fee was paid.

There are only two possible reasons why a counterparty should expose him or herself to the loss that the rentier expects to earn as a profit on the transaction. The first possible reason is that of divergent expectations: the counterparty in this case expects the currency to depreciate, or at least not appreciate by as much as the rentier does. This may be a factor in the willingness of traders to enter into futures contracts, but it is likely to be a marginal one. The theory of efficient markets argues that once private information is made public, prices will come to equal those warranted by the fundamentals determining asset values.[7] In this view, financial derivatives markets should be transitory markets before expectations converge on correct evaluations. Once they do, then rentiers will no longer find counterparties for their transactions in financial futures because, in our example, all of them will wish to buy Deutschmark futures at DM3 per UK£, and the excess demand for these contracts will raise the fee for them to the level that exactly equals the rentier's profit (and the counterparty's loss).

Insofar as there is any truth in this theory it is that financial market expectations converge. This is not so much because traders cognitively realize fundamental values but, more plausibly, because after an exchange of views, of which financial futures trading may be a part, a market consensus emerges.[8] Hence in practice the prices of financial futures instruments are volatile because, as soon as a consensus has formed, the price of any futures contract designed to profit from that consensus view would rise to cover the loss that a counterparty would expect to make. In this situation, financial futures trading would indeed be truly marginal, dependent on quixotic and eccentric sentiments among counterparties, were it not for entrepreneurs whose expectations are formed in industrial and commercial activity rather than in the financial markets, and a third class of traders, namely financial futures brokers or banks. Their mode of operation in the financial futures reveals a second and somewhat more durable reason why a counterparty should expose him or herself to the loss that a rentier expects to earn as a profit on a financial futures contract.

9 The broking of financial futures

Financial futures brokers, or banks, act as intermediaries for entrepreneurs and rentiers, issuing contracts for them and acting as their counterparty. Because of this intermediary function these agents are called banks in this chapter. In general, virtually all modern banks in the advanced capitalist economies trade in some or a variety of financial futures instruments. Like entrepreneurial companies and rentiers, this class of agent is distinguished by the source of its revenue, and its mode of operating in the futures markets. In the previous chapter it was assumed that entrepreneurial companies earn their profits from industrial and commercial activity and use financial futures markets to avoid foreseeable losses, while rentiers earn their profits from investing in financial markets, using financial futures instruments to gain profits. Banks, while they may use financial futures instruments to secure themselves against losses (e.g., using forward interest rate agreements to indemnify themselves against losses on fixed interest loans) principally earn their money in the financial futures markets from the premiums charged for entering into agreements as counterparties with other banks, entrepreneurs and rentiers.

However, as noted above, with unmatched contracts, the rentiers' expected profit, or the expected loss passed on by an entrepreneur, represents an equivalent expected loss to their counterparties, the banks. The only way in which they can avoid this loss is by entering into matched or hedged agreements. In the example used above, if a bank agrees to buy Deutschmarks from the entrepreneur in a year's time at DM3, the bank's expected loss is eliminated by agreeing to sell those Deutschmarks in a year's time, at that same rate to the rentier. A profit may be foregone, but any loss is eliminated and a fee is obtained from both parties. Alternatively, the bank may 'hedge' by finding another bank, rentier or entrepreneur to agree to buy those Deutschmarks at a different rate, perhaps below DM2.50 to make a profit for the bank.

This possibility of eliminating losses by matching or hedging contracts[1] enables the banks to charge a premium that is less than the expected loss on a contract, due to the appreciation or depreciation of the underlying financial asset. Such income from fees, replacing the loan business lost due to the inflation of capital markets[2] is undoubtedly a factor in the enthusiasm of banks in the 1990s for financial futures business. Moreover, whereas the charging of fees equal to the expected loss on a contract would quickly eliminate investors' enthusiasm for the market, the charging of fees less than the expected losses has enabled financial futures markets to flourish in recent years.

So far the discussion in Part III of the book has dealt with a rather simple concept of the price of a futures contract, taking as a representative contract a standard currency future, in order to distinguish between the operations of different classes of agent in the market and to show how the price of a futures contract may be reduced below the expected gain or loss from it. This analysis can be extended in order to distinguish different types of futures contracts according to the degree of competition in their respective markets, and to clarify the process of innovation and the role of diverse expectations in derivatives markets.

Let us suppose that there exists only one financial futures contract in a competitive market. Competition will tend to drive the price of the contract down to the point where the fee or commission for it will barely cover the broker's transaction costs: the risk premium is reduced to the fee for the matching contract through which brokers eliminate their risk. If new brokers are entering the market, then the price may be reduced even below transaction costs, as new brokers try to establish market share by loss-leading, and established brokers accept losses in order to maintain their market share.

Given the common technology of different kinds of futures, in the sense that no new equipment is required to produce a new type of financial future contract, it is profitable for brokers to engage in monopolistic competition by introducing new types of contracts.[3] This may be for a new underlying financial asset, for an established contract at a new maturity date, or for a new value of an underlying asset already traded in financial futures markets. A new contract is brought into the market by a broker who is now in a monopoly position as supplier of that contract and the counterparty to any client who wishes to trade in that contract. This contract is in effect an over-the-counter forward agreement. In essentially faddish markets, the demand for this contract among fund managers and traders may be boosted by its novelty, but it may also be limited if investors expect its market to be less liquid because it is only issued by one broker. Furthermore, because it is less frequently traded among fewer institutions, its future value will be the subject of similarly limited exchanges of market opinion. Expectations concerning the gain or loss from it (e.g., on re-sale or against a hedging transaction in the spot market for the underlying asset) are less likely to converge on a market consensus. The broker's minimum price will therefore be his or her expected loss or the gain foregone.

However, as the contract, or similar contracts, come to be traded among other brokers, two possibilities arise. The first is that a more liquid contract comes to be more easily hedged in the futures market itself. For brokers this means that they can eliminate the risk of being a counterparty to a contract by more immediately issuing a matching contract. This allows brokers to offer the contract at prices below the expected loss or gain foregone. Second, as the contract comes to be more commonly traded, traders arrive more rapidly at a consensus value for the contract.

The relationship between market structure, innovation, the expected values of the underlying assets and prices of futures contracts may be illustrated by means of a simple non-linear equation showing the price of a contract as a function of the difference between a broker's offered contract value of an underlying asset in the future at time t+n ($P^*_{b,t+n}$) and the market's consensus of the value of that underlying asset at time t+n ($P_{b,t+n}$), i.e.,

$$F_{p^*,t+n} = C + (P^*_{b,t+n} - P_{b,t+n})^\sigma \qquad (9.1)$$

$$\sigma \geq 0$$

where $F_{p^*,t+n}$ is the fee or premium for the contract offered, and C is the transaction cost of the contract. σ is a parameter reflecting the degree of competition between brokers in the market for the contract for the underlying asset priced by broker b for maturity at t+n in the future at $P_{*b,t+n}$. If there is perfect competition across the whole range of possible values of $P^*_{b,t+n}$, then σ will equal zero. This would imply that a futures contract could be purchased for the transaction costs of issuing that contract for any future value of the underlying assets.

In the example which is used above, perfect competition would mean that the same (minimal) fee would be charged for converting Deutschmarks in the future at DM3 per UK£ as at DM0.5 per UK£, or at DM100 per UK£. Such an extreme state of affairs could only be brought about because, under the assumptions of perfect competition, namely free entry and exit and numerous firms competing by price in all markets, any broker offering a contract at DM0.5 per UK£ would as easily find a counterparty for a matching or hedging contract as at DM100 per UK£, and would therefore suffer no risk of having to match the contract with a purchase or sale in a cash market where only one exchange rate holds at any one time.

In practice, however, competitive conditions only obtain around the market consensus for the expected value of the underlying asset ($P_{b,t+n}$). Hence σ is in practice greater than zero. A broker making markets across a range of values of P^* expected in time t+n would publish his fees list as a U-shaped function against $P^*_{b,t+n}$ (see Figure 9.1).

The greater the difference between the market consensus view of the future value of the underlying asset and an offered future contract value (or strike price) of that underlying asset, the higher is the fee for the contract, because there is less probability that the broker will be able to hedge with an exactly matching contract. The more competitive are futures markets in the

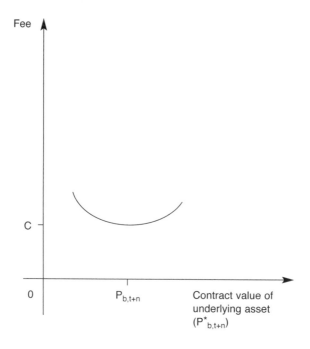

Figure 9.1 Fee (premium) levels against futures contract values (strike price) of an underlying asset.

underlying asset, the flatter will be the curve of function $F^*_{b,t+n}$. However, it should be pointed out that competition does not just depend on the ways in which brokers operate in the market for a particular futures contract. It is also affected by competition in other futures markets. In the first instance, competition in the market for the matching contract affects the broker's ability immediately to lay off all risk by hedging a contract entered into for a client. In other futures markets, the ability to hedge effectively all his other contracts also affects a broker's willingness to price a particular contract competitively. In this sense, competition is a condition of the marketplace in which trade in various contracts takes place, as well as a feature of the particular market for a contract.

This analysis of imperfect competition in financial derivatives trading is important because, contrary to the widespread view that these markets are characterized by a state of competition approaching what economists regard as perfect competition, there is evidence suggesting that markets for financial futures instruments are highly concentrated. For example, an OECD study found that among banks operating in the world's largest futures markets, those of the United States, in 1992 seven derivatives dealers accounted for 90 per cent of all bank derivatives activities.[4] In London, a central banker noted that in 1992 the ten most active principals in financial derivatives had a combined overall share of the market that was 'materially higher' than 43 per cent.[5]

This degree of concentration cannot just be considered as a factor distorting the operations of a price system which would otherwise correspond to that obtaining under perfect competition. It also reflects a peculiarity of financial markets that has a direct bearing on the efficiency of the financial intermediation mechanism, which is considered in greater detail in Chapter 10. In general, firms 'producing' goods and services need to sell those commodities to customers who are not the firms producing the commodities. Car companies, for example, will sell cars to households, governments and companies, but rarely if ever sell their cars to each other. However, the profit that may be obtained from purchasing investment services has a much more universal appeal. Financial instruments are therefore commonly purchased for profit by other firms in the same business, except where market regulation explicitly forbids intermediaries or brokers to act as principals in their market (as for example in the case of stockbroking in the London market before the 1986 reforms). In the case of financial futures, most contracts are intra-market trades between brokers hedging their positions or trading for profit. Precisely what proportion of trades is intra-market is not commonly revealed, but candid traders will informally admit that most of their trade is with other traders as principals.

This has a number of consequences for our understanding of how financial futures markets work. First of all, the figures on the numbers of contracts traded in the various financial futures markets, widely published in comparisons between those markets, are not a reliable indicator of the usefulness of financial futures for the economy in general and retail customers outside the financial futures markets in particular, as is sometimes implied by markets publishing such data. Because of the high share of intra-market trading in total turnover, the published figures on market concentration reveal little about particular firms' share of retail financial markets, and intra-market hedging of retail market exposures.

Second, excess capacity, which is the normal micro-economic mainspring of competition in markets outside the financial system,[6] is smaller in those financial markets where intra-market trading is common. Financial firms which have insufficient retail customers can ensure better utilization of their dealing rooms simply by trading with each other. Moreover, cyclical activity in such markets is not generated by excess capacity but by inflows and outflows of funds.[7]

Third, where excess capacity is kept down in this way, and competition between firms in the financial futures market to find retail customers is correspondingly weak, financial firms tend to orientate their trading strategies towards their more immediate customers in the same business. The result is emulatory competition that is 'conservative in practice and faddish in innovation'[8] and trading for reputation, because reputation gives dealers and their firms market power to influence prices and the pace and direction of innovation. What are commonly called competitive pressures in financial markets are in fact pressures to emulate market leaders, defined by their reputation in the markets. While this may speed the emergence of consensus in particular markets, it may be as much through the exchange of disinformation and rumour as by the exchange of those prices and trading intentions that are the basis of neo-classical theories of financial markets from Walras onwards. Because the business of financial firms is so dependent on reputation among other financial firms, pressures for conformity may seriously inhibit competitive behaviour of the kind envisaged by neo-classical theorists. In particular, the arbitrage which most finance theorists believe keeps prices equal and low in such markets may be confounded by 'reputation premiums' which may allow prestigious firms or markets to maintain higher fees for their services. Competition for reputation among fellow-traders or between markets may also direct innovation towards contracts favoured by other traders in the same business rather than such contracts as are of general social use. Arguably then, the above-cited fragmentary figures on market concentration in financial futures markets understate the degree of imperfect competition in those markets.

10 Regulation and the systemic risk of financial futures

10.1 Regulation and the rise of risk in financial futures markets

Chapters 8 and 9 analysed the operations of financial futures markets according to the type of agent and according to the kind of activity undertaken in the markets. The discussion in those chapters also indicates some of the sources of risk from trading in those markets, and how that risk can be eliminated by hedging and ultimately (and most universally) by liquidity preference. Apart from the problems of systemic and counterparty risk, which affect the whole range of financial markets in some degree, there are essentially two types of risk specific to financial futures. The first is the possibility that a loss will arise because the cash outflow required to settle a futures contract is greater than the cash inflow earned by the economic unit from contracts maturing at the same time, or because the cash inflow generated by the contract is insufficient to cover the cash commitments of the supporting transactions. In the case of difference contracts (specifying the payment of the difference between the actual and the contracted value of a financial parameter), a loss may arise if the difference is not positive or negative as predicted at the time of entering into the contract. So, in our example, the loss would arise if the rentier entered into his or her commitment to buy Deutschmarks at DM3 per UK£, and then found him or herself unable to sell them at any other rate than DM3.50.

The other risk is the much more notional possibility that a profit from movements in a financial parameter will not be realized. So, in our example, this would arise if the entrepreneur found that when the contract to sell Deutschmarks at DM3 per UK£ matured, the exchange rate in the cash market had gone up to DM2.50; or if the rentier discovered that instead of Deutschmarks he or she could have bought for a nominal fee a completely different futures contract to buy Japanese yen at a rate far below the rate in the cash market when the contract matures.

However, in the system described above, there are only two kinds of agents affected by these risks because of their unmatched exposures in the financial futures market: the entrepreneur and the rentier. The entrepreneur uses the futures market to fix the value of a more or less known cash inflow or outflow. The premium that the entrepreneur pays is therefore the price of avoiding a loss in the value of that inflow. In this way, the entrepreneur's cash flow risk is eliminated. The more notional loss of profit from a possibly beneficial movement in financial parameters is an opportunity cost which, in practice, is of marginal interest to entrepreneurs while their current industrial and commercial business earns an adequate return on its capital.

For the rentier, trading in financial futures markets is much more risky. Essentially profits from this trade are made by correctly anticipating future changes in financial parameters against the current market consensus, or by correctly anticipating changes in the current market consensus, so that contracts can be profitably hedged. The source of such profits, and losses, are differences between predicted and historic values in various financial markets. Mathematically, differences are usually more volatile than absolute values or levels.[1] It follows that such losses will usually be less predictable than the underlying financial parameters. This introduces further elements of hazard for rentiers who are not just fixing the value of certain future cash flows but also generating them with claims on other markets. Where futures contracts are in particular commodities (raw materials, or foreign currency, as in our example above) it is common for these contracts to be traded 'on the margin', i.e., a proportion (usually between 10 and 50 per cent) of the contract value has to be deposited with the commission in advance as a token of the purchaser's ability to clear his or her commitments on the due date. Where futures contracts are *differences* between actual and contract values (e.g., in interest rate or stock index futures) only the fee is paid in advance. But in both cases, the initial payment is small in relation to the financial liability or claim that arises when the contract matures, whether or not that liability is profitable or not. This enables a very large number of contracts to be entered into with a relatively small initial outlay, but then requires large gross financial inflows when the contract is settled (see section 10.2 below) whether or not the contracts are profitable.

The small initial outlay is a factor in the rapid expansion of financial futures trading since the 1970s. But it also facilitates a form of 'gambler's frenzy' in the markets: in such hazardous markets a run of losses quickly leads to a large cumulative loss, either because particular contracts may entail huge losses, or because of a large number of small, loss-making contracts. If such a run of losses occurs before one of the regular quarterly settlement days, margin trading can result in a very large settlement charge. A large cumulative loss can only be recovered by a large gain which is usually only to be obtained in such hazardous markets. Hence any loss is an additional incentive to continue to trade.[2] In this way, a trader may continue to accumulate losses until he or she runs out of cash for margin payments. The usual way in which traders employed by banks or rentiers are prevented from succumbing to gambler's frenzy is by limiting the credit that they are allowed to have for margin payments, or placing a ceiling on the value of outstanding contracts that a trader may have at any one time. However, the effectiveness of these measures depends on the integrity of systems for reporting trades and recording them.[3]

A major conclusion of this analysis is that corporate collapses due to trading in financial futures have occurred because industrial and commercial companies and banks have been trading as rentiers, but without the huge cash inflows that immaturity bestows on pension and insurance funds. The conventional justification for this wide participation in the financial futures markets is that the more traders operate in any financial market, the more 'liquid' it is and hence the more it approximates to perfect competition and thereby secures the welfare and equilibrium benefits associated with that state. However, the liquidity of a market is the liquidity of the companies or agents in that market. Companies with limited liquidity may turn over that limited liquidity more rapidly in the financial futures market than they would in their more normal commercial and industrial ventures. But they do not increase their liquidity in the financial futures market unless they consistently accumulate profits in it from other participants who are equally consistently making net payments into the market, an unlikely possibility in view of the hazards of that market.

Two developments have further encouraged entrepreneurs to undertake exposures in excess of those necessary to reduce or eliminate losses due to adverse movements in financial parameters in their normal industrial and commercial business. Low profits from industrial and commercial trading activity make apparently more profitable financial trading activity more attractive to entrepreneurs. This has induced many British and American companies to trade as rentiers in financial futures. At the other extreme, high profits increase the retained liquidity devoted to rentier activities by corporate treasurers. This attracted many Japanese companies to trading as rentiers in financial derivatives at the end of the 1980s.

In the case of banks, trading as rentiers has been induced by the Basle Accord, which requires capital to be set aside against the gross sum of all financial futures exposures.[4] Where capital is scarce then clearly this would limit trading activity. In practice, however, capital markets have expanded very rapidly since the 1970s. Capital has not been scarce for firms operating in financial markets, and the pricing of capital by credit rating gives banks and brokers a strong incentive to engage in risky trading and lending activity: high-rated banks take on more risky business because they have to pay less of the (potentially) high profits to capital owners (i.e., rentiers or institutional investors), who have advanced capital in exchange for lower interest or dividends (because of the perceived lower risk). Low-rated banks *have* to engage in risky activities because this is the only way in which they can earn the high returns required to compensate *their* capital owners for their more risky investment. In this way, the tendency towards over-capitalization increases rather than decreases the hazardous activities of banks, and encourages their involvement in Ponzi financing structures. The latter, as we saw in Chapter 3, offer high returns but also the possibility of large losses.

Moreover, increasing the capital of banks by issuing long-term securities has consequences for the systemic risk in capital markets. Such long-term securities may stabilize bank finances, because they do not need to be rolled over in capital markets that may veer between liquidity and illiquidity. But this is achieved at the expense of increased risk of illiquidity in the capital market in general because banks are less likely to support the market by buying in maturing stock.[5]

In 1996 the Basle Accord was modified to allow banks to set aside capital or reserves only against so-called Value-at-Risk, i.e., the net financial liability or the outstanding liabilities minus claims of a derivatives portfolio given current prices in cash markets, rather than gross liabilities. In modern banking markets where cash and similar reserve items may be bought or sold,[6] this amounts to minimal regulation, except for banks with a poor 'reputation' in inter-bank markets. It also depends on the integrity of the system for reporting outstanding contracts. That integrity is typically weakened in hazardous markets: the larger the loss, the greater is the incentive to evade reporting.

This analysis of how financial futures markets operate has certain implications for regulations to minimize the effects of losses arising out of exposures in financial futures markets. A further rationale for the principles described below, in terms of problems to which any increase in future interest in financial futures markets is likely to give rise, is given in the next section of this chapter.

In general, the efficiency of industrial and commercial companies is reduced when they use financial futures markets in excess of those exposures necessary to insure their industrial and commercial activities against adverse movements in financial parameters. However, discouraging such excess exposure can only be done ultimately by moral injunction because it is not possible to keep a check on the financial market activities of all companies. But forming a climate of business opinion which discourages hazardous speculation in financial markets would undoubtedly help to stabilize company finances.

Second, banks and financial futures brokers, as the counterparties to financial futures contracts, can enhance their financial stability by matching, or hedging all their financial futures contracts in the financial futures market. This can be required as a rule because banks' and brokers' regulators can regularly check the financial futures contracts on their books.

The application of this principle would have two stabilizing and risk-reducing consequences. First, it would make the price system in the financial futures markets work towards the elimination of risk: banks undertaking a net exposure with a corporate or financial client would have to seek another bank or a non-bank client to act as a counterparty for a matching or hedging contract (or contracts). In doing so, they would lower the price of the matching or hedging agreement to make it more attractive to other banks, companies and rentiers. This would therefore make the price mechanism more effective, counteracting the weakening of that mechanism that is implied by the relative absence of excess capacity in financial futures markets.[7]

Second, the matching or hedging of contracts would eliminate the systemic risk arising from the net liabilities of the banking system in respect of financial derivatives contracts, because each bank's and the banking system's overall net exposure would tend to zero. If all bank contracts were matched, or their hedging losses and profits exactly balanced out, then the banking system's net derivatives liabilities would also be zero. By definition, so too would be the net liabilities of companies and rentiers taken together. The price system and the requirement that banks match claims with liabilities would tend to ensure that companies overall had exposures in respect of financial futures that are met by liabilities on the part of rentiers.

The matching of banks' financial futures liabilities would also have a beneficial effect on innovation in financial derivatives markets. This has tended to move towards the development of specialist instruments for particular interests. So, for example, credit insurance (a guarantee that payments on a bank loan will be made during a set period) is bought only by banks. Index futures, guaranteeing compensation for adverse movements in stock market indices, are of interest only to rentier firms and other firms wishing to operate as rentiers. Commodity futures usually are purchased by industrial users of particular commodities. A result of such specialization is that banks may take on liabilities dependent upon price changes in markets in which they may have little practical experience. Banks may be unable to 'lay off' the resulting liability with a matching contract, or unwilling to do so because they believe that they will profit from movements in the financial parameter that their contract has guaranteed. An obligation on banks to match financial futures liabilities would encourage the development of contracts which have a more universal appeal, such as foreign exchange futures. The offering of specialist futures would be discouraged because the fees for them would be forced down by the effective obligation to find an eventual buyer of the counterparty liability outside the banking sector.

Third, rather than banks, as at present, rentiers and any firm wishing to engage in profit-making activity in financial futures markets should be required to maintain minimum liquidity in relation to their proposed exposures and current and future liabilities. In addition to being sufficiently liquid, institutions acting as trustees should have a ceiling placed on the proportion of their investment portfolio that is devoted to financial futures instruments.

Minimum standards of liquidity are implied by the distinction made in Chapter 7 between financial futures which make the profits derived from other activities more certain, and financial futures which add to uncertainty by being the most uncertain source of profit. Where financial futures make a profit more certain, then they can act as a substitute for the accumulation of liquid reserves against an uncertain future. But because most financial futures are employed to obtain very uncertain profits, they require greater amounts of reserves which the speculator may not be able to realize without disturbing other financial markets.

Such principles of regulation go against current conventional thinking in at least three respects. First of all, they distinguish the regulation of companies from that of banks and of professional investors. This is contrary to the current prevailing wisdom that regulations should be the same for all agents (the so-called 'level playing field'). However, the rationale for common regulation is shared hazards because of a common method of operating. It is reasonable to have different regulations for agents operating in different ways and exposed to different kinds of risks.

Second, the principles suggested would raise 'barriers to market entry', which conventional wisdom believes to be anti-competitive and tending to limit the 'liquidity' of the market. In fact, these principles would increase trade in the market since every exposure through a futures contract with a non-bank client would induce subsequent demands by banks for matching or hedging contracts until a matched or hedged contract was agreed with another non-bank client. The encouragement of more widely useful futures contracts would reduce differentiation and perhaps increase the degree of effective competition in these markets.

Finally, with the current fashion for deregulation, it is difficult to make financial regulation more effective. This may be so at the time of writing. But financial markets have always been characterized by cycles of more or less strict regulation, with episodes of financial debauchery (most notably the South Sea and Mississippi Company Bubbles of 1710–20, the gold-mining speculation in the 1900s, and the American stock market bubble of the 1920s) after which stricter regulation has been embraced with relief by all concerned. Each successive corporate collapse, whether or not due to derivatives trading, therefore contributes to a new climate of business opinion favouring tighter regulation. The principles of regulation should be debated in advance of the conjuncture in which they can be implemented, rather than hastily contrived in a crisis, when they are likely to serve particular interests rather than the stability of the market.

10.2 Financial derivatives, institutions and financial fragility

If micro-economic crisis is caused by the draining of liquidity from an individual company (or household)[8] macro-economic crisis or instability, in the sense of a reduction in the level of activity in the economy as a whole, is usually associated with an involuntary outflow of funds from companies (or households) as a whole. Macro-economic instability is a 'real' economic phenomenon, rather than a monetary contrivance, the sense in which it is used, for example, by the International Monetary Fund to mean price inflation in the non-financial economy. Neo-classical economics has a methodological predilection for attributing all changes in economic activity to relative price changes, specifically the price changes that undoubtedly accompany economic fluctuations. But there is sufficient evidence to indicate that falls in economic activity follow outflows of liquidity from the industrial and commercial company sector.[9] Such outflows then lead to the deflation of economic activity that is the signal feature of economic recession and depression. This section examines how financial futures markets may contribute to this kind of macro-economic disturbance.

Such a discussion must start with a consideration of how vulnerable financial futures market themselves are to illiquidity, since this would indicate whether the firms operating in the market are ever likely to need to realize claims elsewhere in order to meet their liabilities to the market. Forced liquidations of this kind were a factor in transforming, for example, the 1929 stock market crash into the 1930s depression.[10]

Paradoxically, the very high level of intra-broker trading is a safety mechanism for the market, since it raises the velocity of circulation of whatever liquidity there is in the market: traders with liabilities outside the market are much more likely to have claims against other traders to set against those claims. This may be illustrated by considering the most extreme case of a futures market dominated by intra-broker trading, namely a market in which there are only two dealers who buy and sell financial futures contracts only between each other as rentiers, in other words for a profit which may include their premium or commission. On the expiry date of the contracts, conventionally set at three-monthly intervals in actual financial futures markets, some of these contracts will be profitable, some will be loss-making. Margin trading, however, requires all the profitable contracts to be fully paid up in order for their profit to be realized. The trader whose contracts are on balance profitable therefore cannot realize his profits until he has paid up his contracts with the other broker. The other broker will return the money in paying up his contracts, leaving only his losses to be raised by an inflow of money. Thus the only net inflow of money that is required is the amount of profit (or loss) made by the traders. However, an accommodating gross inflow is needed in the first instance in order to make the initial margin payments and settle contracts so that the net profit or loss may be realized.

The existence of more traders, and the system for avoiding counterparty risk commonly found in most futures market, whereby contracts are made with a central clearing house, introduce sequencing complications which may cause problems: having a central clearing house avoids the possibility that one trader's default will cause other traders to default on their obligations. But it also denies traders the facility of giving each other credit, and thereby reduces the velocity of circulation of whatever liquidity is in the market. Having to pay all obligations in full to the central clearing house increases the money (or gross inflow) that broking firms and investors have to put into the market as margin payments or on settlement days. This increases the risk that a firm with large net liabilities in the financial futures market will be obliged to realize assets in other markets to meet those liabilities. In this way, the integrity of the market is protected by increasing the effective obligations of all traders, at the expense of potentially unsettling claims on other markets.

This risk is enhanced by the trading of rentiers, or banks and entrepreneurs operating as rentiers, hedging their futures contracts in other financial markets. The hedging of index futures in the stock market gave rise to such coordinated selling in 1987 that stock markets temporarily ceased operations because of insufficient buying interest. However, while such incidents generate considerable excitement around the markets at the time of their occurrence, there is little evidence that they have caused involuntary outflows from the corporate sector on such a scale as to produce recession in the real economy.[11] This is because financial futures are still used by few industrial and commercial companies, and their demand for financial derivatives instruments is limited by the relative expense of these instruments and their own exposure to changes in financial parameters (which may more easily be accommodated by holding appropriate stocks of liquid assets, i.e., liquidity preference[12]). Therefore, the future of financial futures depends largely on the interest in them of the contemporary rentiers in pension, insurance and various other forms of investment funds. Their interest, in turn, depends on how those funds approach their 'maturity'.

Despite the prevalence of widows, pensioners and Belgian dentists in the folklore of the financial markets, the typical contemporary rentier is, as we have noted in Part III, not an individual, but a large pension or insurance fund, or fund managers trading on their behalf. The premium or contributions inflow to these institutions has had an income elasticity significantly greater than unity in recent decades. This is reinforced by a strong contractual element in these inflows, with the result described in Chapter 5 that these funds, since the 1970s, have been 'immature', i.e., premium and contribution inflows have largely exceeded outflows on pensions and insurance claims. To keep down unpredictable liabilities, investments in financial futures, like other highly speculative investments in, say, venture capital or emerging markets, have been limited to small fractions of investment fund portfolios. With rare exceptions, such as the Orange County Pensions Fund collapse in 1994, these institutions have, through their prudence and their fortunate cash flow situation, been able to avoid or absorb cash flow losses in the financial futures markets.

However, the decline of pension fund surpluses poses important problems for the main securities markets of the world where insurance and pension funds are now the dominant investors, as well as for more peripheral markets like emerging markets, venture capital and financial futures. A contraction in the net cash inflow of investment funds will be reflected in a reduction in the funds that they are investing, and a greater need to realize assets when a change in investment strategy is undertaken. In the main securities markets of the world, a reduction in the 'new money' that pension and insurance funds are putting into those securities markets will slow down the rate of growth of the prices in those markets. How such a fall in the institutions' net cash inflow will affect the more marginal markets, such as emerging markets, venture capital and financial futures, depends on how institutional portfolios are managed in the period of declining net contributions inflows.

In general, investment managers in their own firms, or as employees of merchant or investment banks, compete to manage institutions' funds. Such competition is likely to increase as investment funds approach 'maturity', i.e., as their cash outflows to investors, pensioners or insurance policyholders, rises faster than their cash inflow from contributions and premiums, so that there are less additional funds to be managed. In principle, this should not affect financial futures markets, in the first instance, since, as argued above, the short-term nature of their instruments and the large proportion in their business of intra-market trade makes them much less dependent on institutional cash inflows. However, this does not mean that they would be unaffected by changes in the portfolio preferences of investment funds in response to lower returns from the main securities markets. Such lower returns make financial investments like financial futures, venture capital and emerging markets, which are more marginal because they are so hazardous, more attractive to normally conservative fund managers. Investment funds typically put out sections of portfolios to specialist fund managers who are awarded contracts to manage a section according to the soundness of their reputation and the returns that they have made hitherto in portfolios under their management. A specialist fund manager reporting high, but not abnormal, profits in a fund devoted to financial futures, is likely to attract correspondingly more funds to manage when returns are lower in the main markets' securities, even if other investors in financial futures experienced large losses. In this way, the maturing of investment funds could cause an increased inflow of rentier funds into financial futures markets.

An inflow of funds into a financial market entails an increase in liabilities to the rentiers outside the market supplying those funds. Even if profits made in the market as a whole also increase, so too will losses. As was noted above, while brokers commonly seek to hedge their positions within the futures market, rentiers have much greater possibilities of hedging their contracts in another market, where they have assets. An inflow into futures markets means that on any settlement day there will therefore be larger net outstanding claims against individual banks or investment funds in respect of their financial derivatives contracts. With margin trading, much larger gross financial inflows into financial futures markets will be required to settle maturing contracts. Some proportion of this will require the sale of securities in other markets. But if liquidity in integrated cash markets for securities is reduced by declining net inflows into pension funds, a failure to meet settlement obligations in futures markets is the alternative to forced liquidation of other assets. In this way futures markets will become more fragile.

Moreover, because of the hazardous nature of financial futures, high returns for an individual firm are difficult to sustain. Disappointment is more likely to be followed by the transfer of funds to management in some other peripheral market that shows a temporary high profit. While this should not affect capacity utilization in the futures market, because of intra-market trade, it is likely to cause much more volatile trading, and an increase in the pace at which new instruments are introduced (to attract investors) and fall into disuse. Pension funds whose returns fall below those required to meet future liabilities because of such instability would normally be required to obtain additional contributions from employers and employees. The resulting drain on the liquidity of the companies affected would cause a reduction in their fixed capital investment. This would be a plausible mechanism for transmitting fragility in the financial system into full-scale decline in the real economy. But because of the low commitment of pension funds to financial futures trading, with signal exceptions such as the Orange County Pension Fund, its effect is likely to be small. The more probable deflationary mechanism, mentioned in Chapter 6, is the use of companies' internal liquidity to provide liquidity to the capital markets by buying in stock, and tying up liquidity in corporate restructuring and takeover activity.

The proliferation of financial futures markets in the last quarter century has only had been marginally successful in substituting futures contracts for Keynesian liquidity preference as a means of accommodating uncertainty. A closer look at the agents in those markets and their market mechanisms indicates that the price system in them is flawed and trading hazardous risks in them adds to uncertainty rather than reducing it. The hedging of financial futures contracts in other financial markets means that the resulting forced liquidations elsewhere in the financial system are a real source of financial instability that is likely to worsen as slower growth in stock markets makes speculative financial investments appear more attractive. Capital-adequacy regulations are unlikely to reduce such instability, and may even increase it by increasing the capital committed to trading in financial futures. Such regulations can also create an atmosphere of financial security around these markets that may increase unstable speculative flows of liquidity into the markets. For the economy as a whole, the real problems are posed by the involvement of non-financial companies in financial futures markets. With the exception of a few spectacular scandals, non-financial companies have been wary of using financial futures, and it is important that they should continue to limit their interest in financial futures markets. Industrial and commercial companies, which generate their own liquidity through trade and production and hence have more limited financial assets to realize in order to meet financial futures liabilities in times of distress, are more vulnerable to unexpected outflows of liquidity in proportion to their increased exposure to financial markets. The liquidity which they need to set aside to meet such unexpected liabilities inevitably means a reduced commitment to investment in fixed capital and new technology. In this way, the invigoration of finance gives rise to the enervation of industry.

Part IV

Conclusion

11 Ends of finance

This book is about the ends, or purposes, of finance. Underlying it is a view that the general social and economic function of finance, in economic activity outside the financial markets, should determine the value of finance. This is implicit in the methodological approach advanced in Part I of the book, according to which the balance of financial inflows into capital markets determines the value of stocks in those markets. At their most general, these inflows reflect economic activity and the balance between incomes and expenditures, or saving, in the economy at large.

The process of capital market inflation distorts this scheme of economic and social priorities by allowing finance to determine its own values. At this point, the neo-classical theory that the values in capital markets are determined by the productivity of underlying non-financial capital assets in a static economic general equilibrium[1] loses whatever relevance it may have had. Financial futures markets reflect these inverted priorities by enabling participants to speculate on future financial asset values, relative to the market consensus and the financial inflows that determine those values. The social value of the markets is reduced, rather than enhanced, as specialization and innovation proceed in the financial derivatives markets. As was argued in Chapters 7 and 8, non-financial companies can more effectively protect themselves against financial instability by accumulating liquid assets.

The view put forward in this book challenges the implicit conventional wisdom of finance and politics since the 1970s that social and economic policy should have as its principal purpose or end the stability of financial markets. In a period of capital market inflation, such stability can only be precariously purchased by larger and larger inflows into the markets. In Part II it was argued that securities markets dependent on pension and related fund inflows require successive increases in the scope of private pension schemes in order to maintain stability. When the possibilities of such expansion cease, then the markets also cease to be able to finance the social support that is their nominal purpose. This is precisely why pensions and social provision can only be effectively and comprehensively planned and financed by governments.

The discomfort of governments having their monetary policy disrupted by the foreign exchange markets may be cheerfully regarded as another constraint on the venality of the powerful. The ineffectiveness of central banks' anti-inflationary monetary policy, due to companies' replacing their bank borrowing with securities, just as cheerfully punctures a core doctrine of the cult of finance, that only central bankers backed by the confidence of the financial markets can conduct anti-inflationary policy with prudence and integrity. But when the proper conduct of fiscal policy is disturbed because capital markets have to be kept stable, then an irrational policy dilemma has been created in which the ends of finance are raised above all other purposes of civil society. The public institutions supported by fiscal policy hold society together and their expenditure is vital in stabilizing financial flows. These institutions are necessary for the functioning of markets and should not be undermined in the interests of promoting the business of finance and short-term stability in capital markets that are increasingly remote from the proper business of production and distribution.

More importantly, this book has argued that the structure of capital markets is weakened by capital market inflation, which may have nothing to do with the public finances. Instability in capital markets may be treated conservatively along the policy lines advocated by the representatives of finance, through fiscal austerity and high interest rates. But then a process of capital market inflation would require increasing doses of fiscal and mone-tary rectitude until short-term interest rates exceed the prospective returns in the capital market and its speculative bubble is burst. Until inflation is brought to a full stop in such a relatively catastrophic way, such doses will have no effect on those markets' stability, irrespective of the amount of 'cred-ibility' that such rectitude may purchase in the markets. A more active financing policy, the issue of additional government bonds and buying in of such stock in the market when liquidity is low, in the context of greater economic stability, may alleviate the symptoms of capital market inflation more effectively and less catastrophically than bursting speculative bubbles with high interest rates and limitations on lender of last resort facilities.

Moreover, at the heart of the capitalist economy are companies which maintain the economy through their productive activity and investment. The emergence of Ponzi financing structures in the capital market highlights the contradiction between finance as a useful facility for activities outside the capital market, and the need to mobilize the financial resources of house-holds and non-financial companies to support capital market liquidity and values when these are inflated by excessive financial inflows into the markets. With such inflation the capital market ceases to be a useful facility for industrial and commercial companies: the liquidity preference induced by financial uncertainty and over-capitalization discourages such companies from productive investment and makes it easier for them to grow through takeover (merger and acquisition) activity, thereby fuelling the capital market's inflation with their own resources. Today's paragons of industry do not produce and sell commodities in the form of products with an enhanced social use-value. They produce and sell commodities in the form of companies with a capital market value enhanced by inflation in that market. When non-financial companies are drafted in to support the capital markets, by privatization which leaves companies with long-term financial liabilities for past government expenditure, by using company reserves for takeovers (mergers and acquisitions) and share buying schemes, instead of investing those reserves in equipment and technology, it becomes questionable whether they are still carrying out their entrepreneurial functions efficiently or effectively.

If not disturbed by wars or political coups, forcing the markets to close, eras of finance usually come to an end through inflation in the rest of the economy, or in a crisis of withdrawal. If it proceeds more rapidly than the rise in financial asset values, price inflation outside the capital markets may restore a situation in which the capital market obligations of industry and commerce are more normally serviced from their cash flows, rather than from gains obtained from buying and selling financial assets in corporate restructurings designed to realize assets appreciated by capital market inflation. However, such is the fervour of the anti-inflationary mood among economic policy makers at the end of the twentieth century that this relatively benign way of eliminating capital market inflation is unlikely to come about. This leaves the more catastrophic method of capital market disintermediation as the most likely outcome of that market's inflation.

In the past, such crises of withdrawal were discretionary, in the sense that they depended on individual investors' decisions to convert into money their assets in the capital market, even if they may have been forced by their bankers to do so, or by anxiety about a future precipitate fall in the value of those assets. The present era of finance, which has the capital market inflated by pension fund surpluses, is unusual in having that withdrawal spelled out from the very beginning in the terms under which pensions are paid from funded schemes to their beneficiaries. Such collective capital market inflation also institutionalizes the crisis of withdrawal. This makes it easier to put in place strategies to prevent, or rather postpone, such a crisis extending existing pension schemes, or setting up new ones to buy into the market.

In Chapter 6 I put forward the arguments for expecting such an outflow nevertheless to occur. This is because of the progressive maturity of the pension funds that dominate today's securities markets. The conventional pensions projections have put off their maturity well into the next century. However, this maturity is being brought forward or induced by the limited stratum of relatively wealthy individuals who can afford to tie up substantial savings in long-term investments, and the rising preference for immediately accessible savings among companies, households and institutions subject more and more to the vagaries of market forces, and the increasing uncertainty associated with such instability. The end of finance in the sense of a turning away from or disintermediation from securities markets does not mean the end of financial arrangements. Banks will be greatly relieved to resume their former central role in financial intermediation. But those, like pensioners and holders of insurance policies whose wealth and income depend to a greater or lesser extent on values determined in securities markets, will find out to their cost that money paid into securities markets does not stay there 'fructifying' and awaiting withdrawal, but is dispersed outside the market, as implied by the notion of intermediation: the withdrawal of money from securities markets requires inflows of someone else's money, either from companies and governments repaying loans and bonds, or from optimistic investors.

This book also looks forward to the End of the Finance that is an academic discipline guiding the rational choices, among intrinsic capital values, of financial investors, fund managers, governments and corporations. The view that financial markets and their values depend on inflows of funds challenges those theories that regard the market value of financial assets as determined either by the productivity of some underlying real capital asset, or by past market values and fluctuations, or, in 'equilibrium', by both. This is supposed to be secured by competitive mechanisms. However, in spite of their apparently lively and ardently competitive appearance, futures and securities markets are deformed by emulatory competition. Irrespective of the economic value of any underlying capital assets, and rivalry in securities' markets, prices in them are determined, as Cantillon put it, by the amount of money brought to the market. If that money is reduced, or is reversed, then no amount of past inflation or 'productivity' of the underlying assets will raise securities' prices. Past market prices and fluctuations may influence expectations of future gain in markets. But it is the inflow of money through the purchase of securities that enables these expectations to be realized or frustrated. If that inflow declines, after a substantial increase has boosted securities' prices, then the past boom in securities' prices will give way to a fall in prices and the past will have been shown to be a very poor guide to the future. Financial derivatives, far from creating stability, add to this instability the unpredictability of returns from such investments.

Mainstream finance theory starts from the proposition that the supply of funds in the capital markets is made equal to the demand for it by competitive 'market forces', which allocate that supply of funds to the most profitable use in commerce and industry. However, there are no mechanisms at work in the capital markets to ensure that the desired supply of funds is equal to the demand for it. Capital market conjunctures are determined by their antecedents and circumstances, rather then some immanent state of equilibrium. If the inflow of funds is less than the financing requirement of companies (and governments) then the disappointed borrowers resort to the banking system. However, if the inflow of funds is greater than the desired financing of companies and governments, then a process of capital market inflation ensues.

Capital market inflation changes the way in which the capital market works by altering the way in which investors (rentiers) and companies operate in it.

This happens because their respective expectations of gain are changed by the autonomous appreciation of securities prices that capital market inflation creates. Rentiers come to expect gain in the form of increases in the price of their stock, rather than the *income* from that stock. In Keynes's terminology, speculation predominates over enterprise.[2] Increases in stock prices attract more funds to the market, sustaining the original inflation and reinforcing the new habit of earning from capital gains. Investors shift their preferences towards longer-term stocks which appear to be able to secure larger capital gains. An increase in the proportion of their revenue which they obtain from capital gains, rather than dividends or interest, makes financial investors relatively more indifferent to the management of the companies that pay those dividends or interest and more concerned with following conventional speculative trends in order to maximise capital gains.

With capital market inflation it is also easier for companies to secure easy gains from corporate restructuring: buying subsidiaries for subsequent re-sale or flotation in the capital market at a higher price. In a situation of capital market inflation, such profits merely require the services of investment bankers with good connections to fund managers and only a modest degree of good luck. By contrast, the profits from normal trading activities in commerce and industry are much more hazardous: they depend on business cycles, which are more extreme in the absence of government policies to stabilize the economy, and uncertain competition from commercial rivals. With increased willingness by investors to finance business with equity or common stock, companies shift their financing toward stocks which need not be repaid, on which the dividends paid are discretionary, and on which a prospective additional return may be paid by another investor. The stability of capital markets is undermined by the shift to longer term financing requiring market inflation for its continued liquidity.

Orthodox theories of finance dismiss such disequilibrium and its consequences by presumptions of equilibrium and perfect arbitrage. These, in effect, assume perfect liquidity (i.e., an actual ability to sell any amount of stock at or near the going market price of that stock). Such theories do not take into account the structural changes that occur in markets as inflation takes hold: an increase in the average term of stocks reduces the assured liquidity in the market; peripheral markets become liquid through inflows of funds from relatively remote institutions investing speculatively, as a prelude to collapse and illiquidity with any decline in those inflows, while integrated markets, supposed exemplars of perfect capital markets, become more like peripheral markets with the decline of inflows into the investment institutions that have inflated them. With the prospect of illiquidity, rational investor choice is reduced from choosing among investments to timing withdrawals of liquidity from markets. Such systematic shifts in the liquidity of securities markets cannot be accommodated within theories based on equilibrium.

Implicit in this is a critique of the methodology of quantitative analysis in finance, which uses econometric methods to draw inferences about market structure from time series of financial price data. This book argues that such data are the outcome of inflows into the financial markets, but that the crucial structural characteristics of those markets depend on the nature and the networks of claims and obligations being serviced by cash flows into the markets. Such structures are not revealed by financial data, but have to be inferred from the size and type of financial inflow, actual market mechanisms, and changes in financial liabilities. Shifts in market liquidity and abrupt financial crises cannot be predicted nor explained by price changes.

The flaws in the system of capital market finance are not insubstantial shadows, like market 'sentiment' or 'confidence'. Those flaws are inherent in the way in which markets for long-term financial assets operate, but are most fully, if not obviously, incubated when the capital market is inflated. The slower growth of stock prices in the most financially advanced capitalist countries and the financial catastrophes in emerging markets, following fund managers' competition to inflate peripheral markets, suggest that we may be coming towards the end of an era of finance.

Past eras of finance were similarly characterized by a widespread belief in the ability of finance to invigorate business and society, while actually diverting money, organization and labour from the satisfaction of real human and social needs. Past eras of finance ended catastrophically when the inflow of money into financial asset markets dried up because insufficient numbers of wealthy individuals were willing to continue buying assets. The so-called financial suppression that followed the 1929 Crash was a belated, recognition that *laisser-faire* in finance provides too tempting distractions from the real business of business and government, while the burden of excessive liabilities discourages productive enterprise and investment.

In the 1970s, financial *laisser-faire* was released, providing a seemingly endless inflow into capital markets of money by compulsory subscription to pension funds levied on the workforce and their employers. But there is an inherent contradiction between *laisser-faire* and the need to mobilize ever larger inflows into the capital markets. The natural tendency of such inflows to decline is incompatible with low inflation and *laisser-faire* in other markets. In the labour market increasing 'flexibility' makes households require readily accessible liquidity, rather than assets tied up in pension funds, to smooth out the vagaries of markets. Even with full employment, there are still too few people employed in the world on sufficiently high and rising wages to secure steadily rising inflows into securities markets through pension and insurance funds. Perhaps the ultimate irony in all this is that, if the stability of securities markets is to be the end of pension-fund capitalism, then it will take full employment and rising wages, i.e., socialism, to secure it.

Notes

Introduction

1 C. P. Kindelberger, *Manias, Panics and Crashes: A History of Financial Crises* (London, Macmillan, 1989).

2 T. Veblen, *The Theory of Business Enterprise* (New York, Charles Scribner's Sons, 1904), ch. VI and pp. 184–5. I am grateful to Malcolm Rutherford for drawing my attention to Veblen's extraordinarily perceptive work on finance.

3 For example, the most systematic theory of capital market cycles in the second half of the twentieth century was that produced by Hyman P. Minsky. (This is further discussed in this introduction and various chapters of the book.) Minsky, like Veblen, explains financial crisis by postulating a fall in the value of real, productive, capital assets, relative to the value of financial capital assets secured on them, that brings on his financial crisis. He argues that this happens because a Kaleckian business cycle operates autonomously within a finance-dominated capitalist system, and the financial boom coincides with excessive fixed capital investment (see H. P. Minsky, 'The Financial Instability Hypothesis: a restatement', *Thames Papers in Political Economy* (London, Thames Polytechnic, 1978). Veblen's analysis does not need a separate business cycle theory external to his financial cycle theory. He explains the difference between real and financial capital values with an almost Keynesian observation that what he calls 'credit inflation' does not increase demand in the economy proportionately to the increase in financial liabilities (Veblen, op. cit., pp. 109, 209–27).

4 Veblen, op. cit. See also J. P. Raines, and C. G. Leathers, 'Institutional characteristics in the formation of stock prices: the views of Veblen and Keynes', paper presented at the Annual Meeting of the History of Economics Society in Montreal, Canada, June 1998.

5 cf. L. Fishman, 'Veblen, Hoxie and American labor', in D. E. Dowd (ed.) *Thorstein Veblen: A Critical Appraisal* (Ithaca, NY, Cornell University Press, 1958).

6 See T. Veblen, 'The captains of finance and the engineers', in *The Engineers and the Price System*, reprinted in Wesley C. Mitchell (ed.) *What Veblen Taught: Selected Writings of Thorstein Veblen* (New York, The Viking Press 1936).

7 cf. Sweezy's criticism that Veblen did not have a consistent theory of income and expenditure, in P. M. Sweezy, 'Veblen on American capitalism', in Dowd (ed.) op. cit.

8 R. Luxemburg, *The Accumulation of Capital*, translated by Agnes Schwartzschild (London, Routledge and Kegan Paul, 1951). By contrast, Rudolf Hilferding's contemporary Marxist study of finance presented it in a comparatively benign light. Hilferding saw financial crises as confined to the financial system and crises in the real economy as caused by more traditionally

Marxist 'disproportions' in production. But because finance comes to dominate production and concentrates ownership of capital, he regarded it as moderating those disproportions and facilitating the 'socialization of capital': R. Hilferding, *Finance Capital: A Study of the Latest Phase of Capitalist Development*, edited and introduced by Tom Bottomore, translated by Morris Watnick and Sam Gordon (London, Routledge and Kegan Paul, 1981), part IV and pp. 367, 368.

9 I. Fisher, 'The debt deflation theory of great depressions', *Econometrica* 1(1), October 1933: 337–57.

10 Minsky was to write: 'We can assume that the general thrust of Irving Fisher's description ... of the aftermath of a crisis was accepted by Keynes as a rough-and-ready statement of postcrisis system behavior, and that it was assumed implicitly that a symmetrical development occurred during a boom': H. P. Minsky, *John Maynard Keynes*, (New York, Columbia University Press, 1975), p. 64, n. 7. This is inaccurate in that Keynes's analysis of the depression was one of defective demand due to under-investment caused by excessive long-term interest rates, rather than too much debt; and, as Minsky recognizes, Fisher's analysis does not go into the antecedents of over-indebtedness.

11 M. Kalecki, 'Determinants of profits', in *Selected Essays on the Dynamics of the Capitalist Economy 1933–1970* (Cambridge, Cambridge University Press, 1971), ch. 9.

12 M. C. Sawyer, *The Economics of Michał Kalecki* (London, Macmillan, 1985), ch. 2.

13 J. Steindl, *Maturity and Stagnation in American Capitalism* (New York, Monthly Review Press, 1976).

14 H. Magdoff and P. M. Sweezy, *Stagnation and the Financial Explosion* (New York, Monthly Review Press, 1987).

15 C. P. Kindelberger, *World Economic Primacy 1500–1990* (New York, Oxford University Press, 1996).

16 V. Chick, 'The evolution of the banking system and the theory of saving, investment and interest', in P. Arestis, and S. C. Dow (eds.) *On Money, Method and Keynes, Selected Essays* (London, Macmillan, 1992); J. A. Kregel, 'Neoclassical price theory, institutions, and the evolution of securities market organization', *Economic Journal* 105, March 1995: 459–70.

17 cf. 'the banker does not know what he really does or brings about because he cannot observe it ... probably 999 out of 1000 persons working on the stock market do not really know what it does, or how it does it': F. Machlup, *Methodology of Economics and Other Social Sciences* (New York, Academic Press, 1978), pp. 321, 325.

18 See J. Toporowski, *The Economics of Financial Markets and the 1987 Crash* (Aldershot, Edward Elgar, 1993), pp. 46–7.

19 S. C. Dow, *The Methodology of Macroeconomic Thought: A Conceptual Analysis of Schools of Thought in Economics* (Cheltenham, Edward Elgar, 1996), p. 11.

20 Induction reveals plausible propositions. If a hypothesis is plausible then at best statistical verification can only conclude what is already known, namely that the hypothesis is plausible. Only if a hypothesis is entirely implausible, and statistical verification shows that it is consistent with available data, can such procedures add to our knowledge. Insofar as there is any philosophical inspiration behind the academic discipline of finance, it lies in this work of Milton Friedman. Milton Friedman's classic 'positivist' approach to methodology in economics, ignoring plausibility and merely verifying the statistical consistency of predictions, is logical even if its definition of relevant data is extremely narrow. But its author himself, in his own empirical work, shrank from its implied conceptual promiscuity. The most efficient predictors do not necessarily explain anything. See M. Friedman, 'Essay on the methodology of positive economics', in *Essays in Positive Economics* (Chicago, University of Chicago Press, 1953); M. Blaug,

The Methodology of Economics or How Economists Explain (Cambridge, Cambridge University Press, 1980), pp. 103–114; Dow, op. cit., pp. 66–8.

21 European financial trading systems, which only match orders from outside the markets rather than stimulating them with brokers' bids and offers advertised on screen, end up with even less continuous series.

22 cf. 'When, e.g., the putative earning-capacity of the capital covered by a given line of securities, as shown by the market quotations, rises above what is known to its managers to be its actual earning-capacity, the latter may find their advantage in selling out or even in selling short; while in the converse case they will be inclined to buy ... Partial information, as well as misinformation, sagaciously given out at a critical juncture, will go far toward producing a favourable temporary discrepancy of this kind, and so enabling the managers to buy or sell the securities of the concern with advantage to themselves. If they are shrewd business men, as they commonly are, they will aim to manage the affairs of the concern with a view to an advantageous purchase and sale of its capital rather than with a view to the future prosperity of the concern, or to the continued advantageous sale of the output of goods or services by the industrial use of this capital': Veblen, op. cit., pp. 155–6.

23 It is this author's hope that one day someone will write a more definitive and systematic critique of financial statistics in a new edition of Oskar Morgenstern's neglected classic *On the Accuracy of Economic Observations* (second edition, Princeton NJ, Princeton University Press, 1963).

24 This is the objective process underlying the observation known as Goodheart's Law whereby, on becoming a target of monetary policy, a monetary aggregate moves less predictably.

25 Toporowski, op. cit., 73–6.

26 There is a further discussion of these issues in the first part of J. Toporowski 'European destiny and macroeconomic responsibility in the financial systems of Germany and the UK: a balance sheet approach', in S. Frowen (ed.) *Financial Competition, Risk and Responsibility* (London, Macmillan, forthcoming).

27 P. Davidson, 'A post-Keynesian view of theories and causes for high real interest rates', in P. Arestis, (ed.) *Post-Keynesian Monetary Economics: New Approaches to Financial Modelling* (Aldershot, Edward Elgar, 1988), n. 1. Financial analysts have been slow to realize the deeply methodological implications of the health warning which they are now obliged to print in small letters in their advertisements soliciting investment, namely that 'past performance is not a guide to future returns'.

28 Davidson, op. cit. See also M. Kalecki, 'Econometric model and historical materialism', in *On Political Economy and Econometrics: Essays in Honour of Oskar Lange* (Warszawa, Polish Scientific Publishers, 1964).

29 cf. Dow, op. cit., ch. 5.

30 Minsky, *John Maynard Keynes*, Chapter 4.

1 Capital markets and the real economy

1 K. Pilbeam, *Finance and Financial Markets* (London, Macmillan, 1989), pp. 176–7.

2 cf. A. Smith, *An Inquiry into the Nature and Causes of the Wealth of Nations*, Book II (Oxford, Oxford University Press, 1904).

3 Smith, op. cit., p. 390. Smith's enthusiasm for joint stock banking was tempered by his criticism of the credit money notions of his compatriot John Law, whose 'splendid but visionary ideas' may, in Smith's view, 'have contributed to that excess of banking, which has of late been complained of, both in Scotland and in other places' (op. cit., vol. I, p. 354).

4 See J. Toporowski, 'Corporate liquidity, capital markets and their valuation', *Economie Appliquée* tome XLVI, No. 3, 1994 .

5 See J. A. Kregel, *Origini e Sviluppo dei Mercati Finanziari* (Arezzo, Italy, Banca Popolare dell'Etruria e del Lazio/Studi e Ricerche, 1996).

6 See J. M. Keynes, *The General Theory of Employment, Interest and Money*, (London, Macmillan, 1936), pp. 150–1.

7 'The practice, usually considered prudent, by which an investment trust or an insurance office frequently calculates not only the income from its investment portfolio, but also its capital valuation in the market, may also tend to direct too much attention to short-term fluctuations in the latter ... It is said that, when Wall Street is active, at least half of the purchases or sales of investments are entered upon with an intention on the part of the speculator to reverse them the same day. This is often true of the commodity exchanges also ... The spectacle of modern investment markets has sometimes moved me towards the conclusion that to make the purchase of an investment permanent and indissoluble, like marriage, might be a useful remedy for our contemporary evils ... But the liquidity of investment markets often facilitates, though it sometimes impedes, the course of new investment ... The only radical cure for the crises of confidence which afflict the economic life of the modern world would be to allow the individual no choice between consuming his income and ordering the production of the specific capital-asset which, even though it be on precarious evidence, impresses him as the most promising investment available to him': Keynes, op. cit., pp. 157, 160, 161.

8 Smith, op. cit., vol. II, p. 373.

9 See J. A. Kregel, 'Some risks and implications of financial globalization for national policy autonomy', *UNCTAD Review*, 1996.

10 This distinction was originally put forward in M. Kalecki, 'The principle of increasing risk', *Economica* 4, 1937 , and revised as 'Entrepreneurial capital and investment', in *Selected Essays on the Dynamics of the Capitalist Economy 1933–1970* (Cambridge: Cambridge University Press, 1971).

11 For example, Pilbeam, op. cit., p. 14; A. D. Bain, *The Economics of the Financial System* (Oxford, Martin Robertson, 1981). For a good survey of recent theory, that touches upon some of the issues in this book, see I. Grabel, 'Financial markets, the state and economic development: controversies within theory and policy', *International Papers in Political Economy* 3(1) 1996.

12 cf. 'Thus the rate of interest, which is the ratio of net profit to the price of securities, manifests itself in the market for numéraire-capital, that is to say in the banking system, though actually it is determined in the capital goods markets, that is to say the stock exchange, as a rate of net income which is the common ratio of the net price of services to the price of landed capital, personal capital as well as capital proper': L. Walras, *Elements of Pure Economics of the Theory of Social Wealth*, translated by William Jaffé, (London, George Allen and Unwin, 1954), p. 290. See also J. A. Kregel, 'Neoclassical price theory, institutions, and the evolution of securities market organization', *Economic Journal* 105, March 1995: 459–70.

13 See Chapter 2.

14 This hydraulic optimization of investment, implicit in the Washington Consensus view of saving as a prior cause of investment, is the neo-classical equivalent of the crudely Keynesian hydraulic Keynesianism, in which expenditure determines output. See Introduction, pp. 2–3.

15 See Pilbeam, op. cit., p. 14.

16 J.M. Keynes, op. cit., pp. 207–8. I am grateful to Jan Kregel for pointing out this essential characteristic of liquidity.

17 This point is examined further below and in H. P. Minsky, 'The Financial Instability Hypothesis: a restatement', *Thames Papers in Political Economy* (London, Thames Polytechnic, 1978) and *Stabilizing an Unstable Economy* (New Haven, CT, Yale University Press, 1986).

18 In Britain, with the most highly developed stock market in the world in the first half of the century, this led to chronic under-investment in the heavy manufacturing sector. This problem was only resolved by its wholesale nationalization in the 1940s, and state finance of the bulk of fixed capital investment in the British economy. However, by the 1980s, this problematical aspect of capital markets was conveniently forgotten, and nationalized heavy industries were either shut down or privatized. See also Chapter 4.

19 Keynes, op. cit., p. 159.

20 *Committee to Review the Functioning of Financial Institutions: Report* (The Wilson Report), (London: HMSO, 1980) Cmnd 7937, p.132.

21 See W. H. Locke Anderson, *Corporate Finance and Fixed Investment: An Econometric Study* (Cambridge, MA, Harvard University Press, 1964).

22 T. Mott, 'Towards a post-Keynesian formulation of liquidity preference', *Journal of Post-Keynesian Economics* 8, Winter 1985: 222–32; A. S. Eichner and J. Kregel, 'An essay on post-Keynesian theory: a new paradigm in economics', *Journal of Economic Literature* 13, 1975, 1292–394.

23 See Kalecki, op. cit.

24 H. P. Minsky, *John Maynard Keynes* (New York, Columbia University Press, 1975); 'The Financial Instability Hypothesis'; and *Stabilizing an Unstable Economy*. There is a further explanation of Minsky's analysis of financial fragility in Chapter 4.

25 For companies with extensive investment schedules 'what may have been a conservative capitalization ... will become an excessive capitalization after their earning-capacity has declined: T. Veblen, *The Theory of Business Enterprise* (New York, Charles Scribner's Sons, 1904), p. 201.

26 Minsky, *John Maynard Keynes*, ch. 5.

27 See L. R. Wray, 'The political economy of the current US financial crisis', *International Papers in Political Economy* 1(3), 1994.

28 See J. Steindl, *Maturity and Stagnation in American Capitalism* (New York, Monthly Review Press, 1976), p. 121; Kalecki, op. cit.

29 It is only in this special 'equilibrium' case that Minsky's Financial Instability Hypothesis would not apply.

2 Value and excess in capital markets

1 'Les prix se fixent sur les marchés par la proportion des denrées qu'on y expose en vente et de l'argent qu'on y offre pour les acheter': R. Cantillon, Essai sur le nature du commerce en général (Paris, Institut National d'Études Démographiques, 1952 [1755]), p. 7. Richard Cantillon (1680? –1734), an Irish-born French political economist and banker, made a fortune out of company shares in a scheme floated in Paris by a Scottish banker John Law. According to Kindelberger, Cantillon made a profit of 6.5 million livres tournois from the sale of most of his stock in Law's Compagnie d'Occident. Cantillon managed to get most of this profit out of France and into Amsterdam and London just before the collapse of Law's scheme in the summer of 1720. See Chapters 3 and 6.

2 This theory is developed in H. M. Markowitz, 'Portfolio selection', *Journal of Finance* 7(1), 1952, 77–91; *Portfolio Selection: Efficient Diversification of Investment* (New York, John Wiley, 1959); *Mean-Variance Analysis in Portfolio Choice and Capital Markets* (Cambridge, MA, Basil Blackwell, 1990).

3 See F. Black, M. C. Jensen, and M. Scholes, 'The capital asset pricing model:

some empirical tests', in M. C. Jensen (ed.) *Studies on the Theory of Capital Markets* (New York, Praeger, 1972).

4 See R. Roll, and S. Ross, 'An empirical investigation of the arbitrage pricing theory', *Journal of Finance* 35, December 1980.

5 See E. F. Fama, 'Efficient capital markets: a review of theory and empirical work', *Journal of Finance* 25, May 1970.

6 cf. 'If funding generates more money for investment markets than can be turned into real economic investment, it will simply push up prices artificially, as more and more investors chase a limited amount of stock', C. Daykin, *Funding the Future? Problems in Pension Reform* (London: Politeia, 1998), p. 32.

7 See M. Kalecki, 'Determinants of profits', in *Selected Essays on the Dynamics of the Capitalist Economy 1933–1970* (Cambridge, Cambridge University Press, 1971), and J. Toporowski, 'Profits in the UK economy during the 1980s', *Review of Political Economy* 5(1), January 1993.

8 cf. 'The characteristic movement of capital in general, the return of the money to the capitalist, i.e., the return of capital to its point of departure, assumes in the case of interest-bearing capital a wholly external appearance, separated from the actual movement of which it is a form. A gives away his money not as money, but as capital. No real transformation occurs in the capital. It merely changes hands. Its real transformation into capital does not take place until it is in the hands of B [i.e., the entrepreneur]. But for A it becomes capital as soon as he gives it to B. The actual reflux of capital from the processes of production and distribution takes place only for B. But for A the reflux assumes the same form as the alienation. The capital returns from B to A. Giving away, i.e., loaning money for a certain time and receiving it back with interest (surplus value) is the complete form of the movement peculiar to interest-bearing capital as such. The actual movement of loaned money as capital is an operation lying outside the transactions between lender and borrower. In these the intermediate act is obliterated, invisible, not directly included ...': Karl Marx, *Capital Volume III: The Process of Capitalist Production as a Whole* (Moscow, Progress Publishers, 1959), p. 348. Keynes is said to have spoken with approval of Marx's notion of 'circuits' of capital and used the idea in his *A Treatise on Money in Two Volumes* (London, Macmillan, 1930). See also A. Graziani, 'The theory of the monetary circuit', *Thames Papers in Political Economy* (London, Thames Polytechnic, 1989).

9 See A. D. Bain, *The Economics of the Financial System* (Oxford: Martin Robertson, 1981), pp.12–13.

10 See J. Tobin, 'A general equilibrium approach to monetary theory', *Journal of Money, Credit and Banking* 1(1), February 1969, 322–38. If Tobin's theory were correct, the world would have experienced a phenomenal fixed capital and technology investment boom with the capital market inflation since the 1970s. (The absence of one is further discussed in Chapter 3).

11 Keynes had reflected on this at the time of the 1929 Crash, when he wrote that 'bear' views in stock markets have 'the result of augmenting the demand for money in financial circulation' (i.e., in the financial system). J. M. Keynes, *A Treatise on Money in Two Volumes. 1 The Pure Theory of Money*, p. 290.

12 See Toporowski 'The financial system and capital accumulation in the 1980s', in F. Green (ed.) *The Restructuring of the UK Economy* (Hemel Hempstead, Harvester Wheatsheaf, 1989); *The Economics of Financial Markets* (Aldershot: Edward Elgar, 1993); 'Corporate liquidity, capital markets and their valuation', *Economie Appliquée* tome XLVI, No. 3., 1994.

13 See Toporowski, 'Corporate liquidity'.

14 See Toporowski, *The Economics of Financial Markets*, ch. 3.

15 See World Bank, *The World Development Report 1989* (New York, Oxford University Press for the World Bank, 1989).

16 E. S. Shaw, *Financial Deepening in Economic Development* (New York, Oxford University Press, 1973), pp. 3–4.

17 cf. J. Steindl, *Small and Big Business: Economic Problems of the Size of Firms* (Oxford, Basil Blackwell, 1945), ch. IV.

18 A leading theorist of the 'financial repression' school, Maxwell Fry, himself admits that capital markets are of little use in developing countries: in those countries 'at best stock markets play a minor role; more often they resemble gambling casinos and may actually impede growth in developing countries' (M. Fry, 'In favour of financial liberalization', *The Economic Journal* 107(442), May 1997, 754–70). After the financial crises of Mexico in 1994 and the Far East in 1997, many followers of McKinnon and Shaw, like Fry, have tended to restrict their liberalizing zeal to banking.

19 'Takeovers normally result in the replacement of the management of the company that is taken over. The threat of takeover should encourage the management to make the firm efficient. To the extent that such forces are in play, the stockmarket encourages efficiency and profitability of firms and thereby benefits the economy': K. Pilbeam, *Finance and Financial Markets* (London, Macmillan, 1989), p. 176. A less friendly commentator notes that 'the stock market ... is best thought of as a way of organizing the ownership and control of the means of production – a vehicle for the buying and selling of whole corporations ...': D. Henwood, 'The stock market and the economy', *Review of Radical Political Economy* 29(4), 1997, 144–8, p. 147. See also 'A survey of capitalism', *Economist*, 5 May 1990.

20 The Bank of England has periodically issued warnings against excessive debt finance during takeover booms in the first half of the 1970s and in the second half of the 1980s. For general reviews of the issues, see J. Carty *et al.*, 'Takeovers and short-termism in the UK', *Industrial Policy Paper No. 3* (London, Institute for Public Policy Research, 1990), and P. Marsh, *Short-termism on Trial* (London, Institutional Fund Managers' Association, 1990). There is further discussion of these issues in Chapter 3.

21 'Thus the remedy for the boom is not a higher rate of interest but a lower rate of interest': J. M. Keynes, *The General Theory of Employment, Interest and Money*, (London, Macmillan, 1936), p. 322.

22 See Toporowski, *The Economics of Financial Markets*, ch. 3.

23 In the 1980s, privatization offered a temporarily much more effective way of removing some of the excess liquidity in the capital market. See Chapter 4.

24 Keynes, *The General Theory*, p. 160.

3 Pension funds and Ponzi finance

1 E.g., Organization for Economic Co-operation and Development (OECD), 'Ageing in OECD countries: a critical policy challenge', *Social Policy Studies no. 20* (Paris, OECD, 1996); D. Mabbett, 'Pension funding: economic imperative or political strategy?', *Discussion Paper Series No. 97/1* (Uxbridge, Department of Government, Brunel University, 1997); E. P. Davis, *Pension Funds, Retirement Income, Security and the Development of Financial Systems: An International Perspective* (Oxford, Clarendon Press, 1997).

2 Such underlying industrial torpor, and the emergence of pension and insurance funds as the rentiers of our time, was recognized at the beginning of the 1980s by the Austrian economist Josef Steindl. See J. Steindl, 'The role of household saving in the modern economy', *Banca Nazionale del Lavoro Quarterly Review* 140, March 1982, reprinted in J. Steindl, *Economic Papers 1941–88* (London, Macmillan, 1990).

3 cf. N. Kaldor, *The Scourge of Monetarism* (Oxford, Oxford University Press, 1982).

4 cf. C. A. E. Goodhart, 'Financial innovation and monetary control', *Oxford Review of Economic Policy* 2(4),Winter 1986, 79–102.

5 E.g. F. A. Hayek, *Prices and Production* (New York, Augustus M. Kelly, 1935), lecture III.

6 cf. C. A. E. Goodhart, *Monetary Theory and Practice: The UK Experience* (London, Macmillan, 1984).

7 See Chapter 1 and Toporowski, *The Economics of Financial Markets* (Aldershot, Edward Elgar, 1993), ch. 3.

8 See Chapter 5.

9 J. M. Keynes, *The General Theory of Employment, Interest and Money* (London, Macmillan, 1936) p. 197.

10 Keynes, op. cit. p. 151, n. 1.

11 H. P. Minsky, *John Maynard Keynes* (New York, Columbia University Press, 1975) and 'The Financial Instability Hypothesis: A restatement', *Thames Papers in Political Economy* (London, Thames Polytechnic, 1978).

12 It was from Keynes's similar analysis of fixed capital investment by entrepreneurs that Minsky appears to have developed this view of financial speculation. See Minsky, *John Maynard Keynes*.

13 E. Streisler 'Structural economic thought: on the significance of the Austrian School today', *Zeitschrift für Nationalökonomie* 29, 1969, 237–66. See also Chapter 7.

14 Minsky, 'The Financial Instability Hypothesis', p. 24.

4 Capital market inflation and privatization

1 See World Bank, *The World Development Report 1989* (New York, Oxford University Press for the World Bank, 1989).

2 The view of privatization as a 'zero-cost' transfer of government liabilities to the private sector is given in C. Andrade, 'Telecommunications privatisation in Britain and France: increased efficiency or pragmatism', dissertation submitted for the degree of MA in Applied European Studies, South Bank University, London, January 1998. The silence over the matter of privatization on the part of the devotees of the doctrine that government bond issues 'crowd out' private sector finance is an eloquent testimony to the ideological power of finance.

3 See J. Toporowski, 'Financial fragility in the banking systems of transitional economies in Eastern Europe', in S. Sharma (ed.) *Restructuring Eastern Europe: The Microeconomics of the Transition Process* (Cheltenham, Edward Elgar, 1997) and 'Capital market inflation and privatisation in capitalist and post-communist economies', *Zagreb International Review of Economics and Business*, 1(2), 1998, 77–89.

4 This is an identity equation derived from the sectoral accounts for an economy as a whole, and showing that the savings in the economy are by definition equal to the gross fixed capital formation (or fixed capital investment) plus the government's fiscal deficit, plus the foreign trade surplus. See Chapter 2, section 2.1.

5 Replacing the household sector deficit with capitalists' consumption, minus saving out of wages, gives Kalecki's profits function. See Chapter 2 and J. Toporowski, 'Profits in the UK economy during the 1980s', Review of Political Economy 5(1), January 1993, 65–84 and M. Kalecki, 'Determinants of profits' in *Selected Essays on the Dynamics of the Capitalist Economy 1933–1970* (Cambridge, Cambridge University Press, 1971).

6 See Chapter 2, n. 1.

7 Writing at the time of scandals associated with the East India Company, Adam Smith took a characteristically dim view of the flotation of joint stock companies for foreign trade, like the Mississippi and South Sea Companies: they 'have seldom succeeded without an exclusive privilege; and frequently have not

succeeded with one. Without an exclusive privilege, they have commonly mismanaged the trade. With an exclusive privilege, they have both mismanaged and confined it', A. Smith, *An Inquiry into the Nature and Causes of the Wealth of Nations*, Vol. II (Oxford, Oxford University Press, 1904), pp. 373–4). Smith may therefore have taken a very different view of privatization to that of his latter-day acolytes.

8 Details of these exciting financial innovations are given in A.E. Murphy, *John Law: Economic Theorist and Policy-Maker* (Oxford, The Clarendon Press, 1997).

9 Murphy, op. cit. pp. 190–3.

5 Pension fund inflows and their investment

1 In the US in 1980, 17.5 million individuals contributed to private 'defined contribution' pension plans. In 1995, 42 million Americans were contributing to such schemes (David Hale, 'Our mutual revolution', *Financial Times,* 22 April 1998). It should be noted that a society like the US with net immigration by adults of working age is correspondingly less likely to experience maturity of the funded pension system as a whole, providing that pension outflows can be balanced by increases in employment and wages. See Chapter 6.

2 'A projection of occupational pension schemes to the end of the century', paper by the Government Actuary's Department, Appendix 5 of Committee to Review the Functioning of Financial Institutions 1980.

3 'World economy', *Financial Times* Survey, 7 October 1995, p. 8.

4 The special situation of Hong Kong is detailed in C. Chan 'China: foreign capital and economic instability under the "one country two systems" policy', dissertation submitted for the degree of MSc in International Business, London, South Bank University, 1997.

5 See Chapter 3, section 3.3.

6 See World Bank, *Global Economic Prospects and Developing Countries* (Washington, DC, World Bank, 1997).

7 There is now a considerable literature documenting this phenomenon. See J. A. Kregel, 'Some risks and implications of financial globalization for national policy autonomy', *UNCTAD Review,* 1996; I. Grabel 'Financial markets, the state and economic development: controversies within theory and policy', *International Papers in Political Economy* 3(1), section 4; A. Singh 'Financial liberalization, stock markets and economic development', *The Economic Journal* 107(442), May 1997, 771–82; S. Griffith-Jones with J. Cailloux and S. Pfaffenzeller, 'The East Asian financial crisis: a reflection on its causes, consequences and policy implications', *IDS Discussion Paper* No. 367 (Brighton, University of Sussex, 1998); A. J. Juric, 'The contagion effect of the East Asian crisis on Eastern Europe', dissertation submitted for the degree of MA in European Studies, London, South Bank University, 1998.

8 See Chapter 3, section 3.3.

9 See J. Toporowski, *The Economics of Financial Markets and the 1987 Crash* (Aldershot, Edward Elgar, 1993), pp. 126–32.

10 Ibid., pp. 127–30.

11 cf. Juric, op. cit., and Griffith-Jones, op. cit.

6 The end of funded pension schemes

1 There is no corresponding increase in the expenditure of depositors, receiving higher interest income, since the latter have a lower propensity to spend than indebted households and firms. See also section 3.2 of Chapter 3.

2 See World Bank, *Averting the Old Age Crisis: Policies to Protect the Old and Promote Growth*, World Bank Policy Research Report (New York, Oxford University Press, 1994) and 'A survey of the economics of ageing', *Economist*, 27 January 1996.

3 This is further explained in Chapter 7. This kind of liquidity preference, or desire for more rapid and easy access to the cash value of a given stock of savings, should be distinguished from precautionary saving, that is additional saving (and hence reduced expenditure) undertaken in anticipation of reduced income. Keynes's analysis, in terms of the liquidity preference of wealthy investors, is given in J. M. Keynes, *The General Theory of Employment, Interest and Money* (London, Macmillan, 1936), pp. 170–2, 196. See also note 4.

4 cf. 'What is perhaps still more decisive against thrift on the part of workmen is the fact that the modern large organization of industry requires a high degree of mobility on the part of employees. It requires, in fact, that the labour force and the labour units be mobile, interchangeable, distributable, after the same impersonal fashion as the mechanical contrivances are movable and distributable. The working population is required to be standardized, movable, and interchangeable in much the same impersonal manner as the raw or half-wrought materials of industry. From which it follows that the modern workman cannot advantageously own a home. By force of this latter feature of the case he is discouraged from investing his savings in real property, or, indeed, in any of the impedimenta of living. And the savings-bank account, it may be added, offers no adequate substitute, as an incentive to thrift, in the place of such property as a dwelling-place, which is tangibly and usefully under the owner's hand and persistently requires maintenance and improvement ... The conditions of life imposed upon the working population by the machine industry discourage thrift': T. Veblen, *The Theory of Business Enterprise* (New York, Charles Scribner's Sons, 1904), pp. 325–6). Paradoxically, the welfare state has provided much of the financial security that has allowed home ownership to proliferate. But the decline of state pension schemes is placing pension provision among those 'impedimenta of living' from which working people are increasingly excluded by financial insecurity.

5 If the view put forward in this book is correct, then paying bonuses related to increases in stock prices or stock options to senior managers would seem to be illogical and perverse: illogical because changes in stock prices may have nothing to do with the sound management of a company, but may be caused by capital market inflation which, as it proceeds, makes changes in stock prices even less related to good company management; and perverse because stock options are an incentive to senior managers to spend their company's resources non-productively on measures to win investors' affections, from 'road shows' to fees for retaining the services of prestigious and well-connected investment bankers. At their most perverse, such schemes may encourage Ponzi finance in companies with programmes to buy in stock (to keep stock prices high) using borrowed money. A recent report revealed that 'total remuneration for the chief financial officers for the [United States'] largest 350 companies rose 97.11 per cent during 1996, to an average of $2.99m (£1.79m). Stock option programmes were chiefly responsible, with exercised options alone accounting for slightly more than half (50.58 per cent) of total remuneration ... The best paid officer was Mr. Rollin Dick, of Conseco, an Indiana-based life assurance holding company. He received $12.84m ... of which only $4.96m came from his salary and bonus. His total pay rose by 249 per cent. Conseco has been one of several companies to lead the consolidation of the life assurance industry, making more than 20 acquisitions in the current decade. Its share price out-performed all other life insurers. Its chief executive, Mr. Stephen Hilbert, is also committed to an aggressive

programme of buying stock for employees, with a target that all staff should have
a stake in the company' (*Financial Times*, 28 July 1998).

7 Liquidity preference and the conventional approach to financial futures

1 Philip York, Earl of Hardwick (ed.) *Miscellaneous State Papers from 1501 to
1726*, Vol. II (London, W. Strahan and T. Cadell, 1778), p. 589.
2 Apart from his financial schemes, Law is nowadays best known for advocating
the use of bank credit as money instead of specie (gold or silver). Since the US
dollar was taken off the gold standard in 1971, bank credit has become the virtually universal form of money. See J. Law, *Money and Trade Considered: With a
Proposal for Supplying the Nation with Money* (Glasgow, R. and A. Foulis, 1750).
3 A. E. Murphy, *John Law: Economic Theorist and Policy-maker* (Oxford, The
Clarendon Press, 1997), pp. 241–2.
4 J. M. Keynes, *The General Theory of Employment, Interest and Money*, (London,
Macmillan, 1936), chs 15, 23, and 'The general theory of employment', *Quarterly
Journal of Economics* 51, 1937. Minsky puts a somewhat different gloss on
Keynes's work by reading into it a theory of fragile financial structures, rather
than of excessive interest rates and entrepreneurial irresoluteness: H. P. Minsky,
John Maynard Keynes (New York, Columbia University Press, 1975).
5 See T. M. Rybczyński 'Financial systems and industrial restructuring', *National
Westminster Bank Quarterly Review*, November 1988.
6 P. Davidson, 'A post-Keynesian view of theories and causes for high real interest
rates', in P. Arestis, (ed.) *Post-Keynesian Monetary Economics: New Approaches
to Financial Modelling* (Aldershot, Edward Elgar, 1988). See also P. Davidson
'Are grains of sand in the wheels of international finance sufficient to do the job
when boulders are often required?', *The Economic Journal* 107(442), May 1997,
672–86 and A. Imperato, *Informazione Aspettative ed Incertezza* (Napoli:
Edizione Scientifiche Italiane, 1997), ch. 2.
7 Committee on Banking Regulations and Supervisory Practices, *Proposals for
Institutional Convergence of Capital Measurements and Capital Standards:
Consultative Paper* (Basle, Bank for International Settlements, 1987).
8 Keynes, *The General Theory*, pp. 152–61.
9 The Cox-Ross formula for valuing options allows volatility to vary in proportion
to the price of the asset.
10 See F. Black 'How to use the holes in Black-Scholes', *The Continental Bank
Journal of Applied Corporate Finance* 1, Winter 1989, 67–73.
11 A similar formula is given in Davidson, 'Are grains of sand …?'.
12 H. M. Markowitz, *Mean-Variance Analysis in Portfolio Choice and Capital
Markets* (Cambridge, MA, Basil Blackwell, 1990).
13 See Introduction and Part I.
14 Fischer Black obituary in *Financial Times*, 2 September 1995. His obituary in
the *Economist* revealed that within a year of publishing his 1973 paper on the
valuation of options, Texas Instruments was advertising in the *Wall Street
Journal* that 'You can find the Black-Scholes value using our calculator'
(*Economist,* 9 September 1995). On the possibility of using such probabilistic
methods of estimating future values, Keynes remarked that the 'conventional
method of calculation will be compatible with a considerable measure of stability in our affairs, *so long as we can rely on the maintenance of our convention …*
Thus investment becomes reasonably "safe" for the individual investor over short
periods, and hence over a succession of short periods however many, if he can
fairly rely on there being no breakdown in the convention and on his having an
opportunity to revise his judgement and change his investment, before there has
been time for much to happen': Keynes, *The General Theory*, pp. 152–3.

15 F. Allen and G. Gorton 'Churning bubbles', *Review of Economic Studies* 60(4),. 1993, 813–36; S. Bikhchandani, D. Hirshliefer and I. Welch, 'A theory of fads, fashion, custom and cultural change as informational cascades', *Journal of Political Economy* 100(5), 1992, 992–1026; D. Hsieh 'Chaos and non-linear dynamics: application to financial markets', *Journal of Finance* 46(5), 1991, 1839–1877.

16 A definition of statsbabble is given in Chapter 1, p. 41. A recent study showed that the company analysts who are employed by brokers do not understand much of the data which they circulate, but that their priority is 'to get earnings news to fund managers at speed ... because, in the long run, this [service] can help generate commission income': (J. Kelly, 'Power of magic numbers', *Financial Times*, 2 July 1998. Reading press reports is a useful antidote against an excessive belief in what is widely supposed to be the infallibility of market traders' insights, if only because financial journalists also make much of the infallibility of their own market insights. Journalists and traders establish their reputations by making their respective insights coincide. When this happens, a conventional wisdom is born that can be as ephemeral and vacuous as it is self-regarding. For example, 'why did the latest rally in the (short sterling futures) contracts only occur yesterday? After all, traders knew the day before that Mr. Kenneth Clarke, the U.K. Chancellor, had left base rates unchanged because the pound was strong. Mr. Philip Uglow, economist at Union Discount in London, said: "Sometimes the markets wait overnight to see what the newspapers will say about the data"': *Financial Times*, 8 February 1997.

17 See Chapter 8.

8 Commercial and investment uses of financial futures

1 J. Toporowski, *The Economics of Financial Markets and the 1987 Crash* (Aldershot, Edward Elgar, 1993), pp. 63–8. When the organic structures of cause and effect that give rise to changes in financial markets are obscured by probabilistic conjectures, investment in financial futures appears indistinguishable from gambling. Accordingly, in April 1998, a court in Moscow ruled that 'some forward contracts were best viewed as gambling contracts under chapter 58 of the Russian civil code, and were therefore not enforceable under local law': *Financial Times*, 6 July 1998.

2 See Chapter 1 and Toporowski, op. cit., ch. 3.

3 cf. P. Davidson, 'Are grains of sand in the wheels of international finance sufficient to do the job when boulders are often required?', *The Economic Journal* 107(442), May 1997, 672–86.

4 This is reflected in Keynes's 'beauty contest' theory of investment or speculation. See Toporowski, op. cit., pp. 115–17; and the Introduction above.

5 See Introduction and Chapter 1.

6 Toporowski, op. cit., pp. 120–7.

7 See Chapter 5 and E. F. Fama, 'Efficient capital markets: II', *Journal of Finance* 46(5), 1991, 1575–617.

8 Toporowski, op. cit., pp. 113–17.

9 The broking of financial futures

1 This kind of risk management is described in B. Steil, 'Regulatory foundations for global capital markets', *Finance and the International Economy: The Amex Bank Review Prize Essays* 6, 1992.

2 See Chapter 3.

3 J. Toporowski, *The Economics of Financial Markets and the 1987 Crash* (Aldershot, Edward Elgar, 1993), pp. 51–2.
4 Organisation for Economic Co-operation and Development, *The New Financial Landscape* (Paris, OECD, 1995).
5 B. Quinn, 'Derivatives – where next for supervisors?', *Bank of England Quarterly Bulletin* 33(4), November 1993, 535–8.
6 See J. Steindl, *Maturity and Stagnation in American Capitalism* (New York, Monthly Review Press, 1976), part I.
7 See Chapter 10, section 10.2, and Toporowski, op. cit., ch. 5.
8 Toporowski, op. cit., p.52.

10 Regulation and the systemic risk of financial futures

1 Over a long period, the variance of the difference equals twice the variance of levels minus twice the covariance of successive observations. Only if that covariance is high will the variance of the difference be greater than the variance of levels.
2 J. Toporowski, *The Economics of Financial Markets and the 1987 Crash* (Aldershot, Edward Elgar, 1993), p. 119.
3 There is evidence that such systems were evaded allowing huge losses to accumulate at Metallgesellschaft and Barings Bank. In the case of Metallgesellschaft, no less an authority than the Nobel Laureate Merton Miller assured the public that the loss-making trading strategy, if it had continued, would have covered its losses and recorded a profit (*Economist*, 1 October 1994).
4 cf. B. Steil, 'Regulatory foundations for global capital markets', *Finance and the International Economy: The Amex Bank Review Prize Essays* 6, 1992.
5 See Chapter 2, section 2.2.
6 See V. Chick, 'The evolution of the banking system and the theory of saving, investment and interest', in P. Arestis, and S. C. Dow (eds.) *On Money, Method and Keynes, Selected Essays* (London, Macmillan, 1992).
7 See Chapter 9, pp. 117–18.
8 See Chapter 1 and Chapter 8, section 8.1.
9 C. P. Kindelberger, *A Financial History of Western Europe* (Oxford, Oxford University Press, 1993), ch. 15; H. P. Minsky, *Stabilizing an Unstable Economy* (New Haven, CT, Yale University Press, 1986), ch. 9 and *John Maynard Keynes*, (New York, Columbia University Press, 1975) ch. 6; H. M. Hyndman *Commercial Crises of the Nineteenth Century*, with a new preface by John A. Hobson, Reprints of Economics Classics (New York, Augustus M. Kelly Publishers, 1967); Toporowski, op. cit., ch. 5.
10 J.K. Galbraith, *The Great Crash 1929* (London, André Deutsch, 1980), pp. 179–80.
11 Toporowski. op. cit., ch. 8.
12 See Chapter 8, section 8.1.

11 The ends of finance

1 L. Walras, *Elements of Pure Economics of the Theory of Social Wealth*, translated by William Jaffé, (London, George Allen and Unwin, 1954), p. 290.
2 J. M. Keynes, *The General Theory of Employment, Interest and Money* (London, Macmillan, 1936), pp. 158–9.

Bibliography

Allen, F. and Gorton, G. (1993) 'Churning bubbles', *Review of Economic Studies* 60(4): 813–36.

Anderson, W. H. Locke (1964) *Corporate Finance and Fixed Investment: An Econometric Study*, Cambridge, MA: Harvard University Press.

Andrade, C. (1998) 'Telecommunications privatisation in Britain and France: increased efficiency or pragmatism', dissertation submitted for the degree of MA in Applied European Studies, London: South Bank University.

Arestis, P. (ed.) (1988) *Post-Keynesian Monetary Economics: New Approaches to Financial Modelling*, Aldershot: Edward Elgar.

Arestis, P. and Demetriades, P. (1997) 'Financial development and economic growth: assessing the evidence', *Economic Journal* 107(442), May: 783–99.

Bain, A. D. (1981) *The Economics of the Financial System*, Oxford: Martin Robertson.

Bikhchandani, S., Hirshliefer, D. and Welch, I. (1992) 'A theory of fads, fashion, custom and cultural change as informational cascades', *Journal of Political Economy* 100(5), October: 992–1026.

Black, F. (1989) 'How to use the holes in Black-Scholes', *The Continental Bank Journal of Applied Corporate Finance* 1, Winter: 67–73.

Black, F., Jensen, M. C. and Scholes, M. (1972) 'The capital asset pricing model: some empirical tests', in M. C. Jensen (ed.) *Studies on the Theory of Capital Markets*, New York: Praeger.

Blaug, M. (1980) *The Methodology of Economics or How Economists Explain*, Cambridge: Cambridge University Press.

Cantillon, R. (1952) [1755] *Essai sur le nature du commerce en général*, Paris: Institut National d'Études Démographiques.

Carty, J., Cosh, A., Hughes, A., Plender, J. and Singh, A. (1990) 'Takeovers and short-termism in the UK', *Industrial Policy Paper* No. 3, London: Institute for Public Policy Research.

Chan, C. (1997) 'China: foreign capital and economic instability under the "one country two systems" policy', dissertation submitted for the degree of MSc in International Business, London: South Bank University.

Chick, V. (1986) 'The evolution of the banking system and the theory of saving, investment and interest', in P. Arestis and S. C. Dow (eds.) *On Money, Method and Keynes, Selected Essays*, London: Macmillan, 1992.

Committee on Banking Regulations and Supervisory Practices (1987) *Proposals for*

*institutional convergence of capital measurements and capital standards.
Consultative Paper*, Basle: Bank for International Settlements.

Committee to Review the Functioning of Financial Institutions: Report (The Wilson
Report) (1980) Cmnd 7937, London: HMSO.

Davidson, P. (1988) 'A post-Keynesian view of theories and causes for high real interest rates', in P. Arestis (ed.) *Post-Keynesian Monetary Economics: New Approaches
to Financial Modelling*, Aldershot: Edward Elgar.

—— (1997) 'Are grains of sand in the wheels of international finance sufficient to do
the job when boulders are often required?', *Economic Journal* 107(442), May:
671–86.

Davis, E. P. (1997) *Pension Funds, Retirement Income, Security and the Development
of Financial Systems: An International Perspective*, Oxford: Clarendon Press.

Daykin, C. (1998) *Funding the Future? Problems in Pension Reform*, London: Politeia.

Dow, S. C. (1996) *The Methodology of Macroeconomic Thought: A Conceptual
Analysis of Schools of Thought in Economics*, Cheltenham: Edward Elgar.

Economist (1990) 'A survey of capitalism', 5 May.

Economist (1994) 'Gunning for Metall', 1 October: 121.

Economist (1996) 'A survey of the economics of ageing', 27 January.

Eichner, A. S. and Kregel, J. (1975) 'An essay on post-Keynesian theory: a new paradigm in economics', *Journal of Economic Literature* 13: 1293–314.

Fama, E. F. (1970) 'Efficient capital markets: a review of theory and empirical work',
Journal of Finance 25, May: 383–417.

—— (1991) 'Efficient capital markets: II', *Journal of Finance*, 46(5), December:
1575–617.

Fisher, I (1933) 'Debt deflation theory of great depressions', *Econometrica* 1(1),
October: 337–57.

Fishman, L. (1958) 'Veblen, Hoxie and American Labor', in D. E. Dowd (ed.)
Thorstein Veblen: A Critical Appraisal, Ithaca, NY: Cornell University Press.

Friedman, M. (1953) 'Essay on the methodology of positive economics', in *Essays in
Positive Economics*, Chicago, IL: University of Chicago Press.

Fry, M. J. (1997) 'In favour of financial liberalization', *Economic Journal* 107(442),
May: 754–70.

Galbraith, J. K. (1980) *The Great Crash 1929*, London: André Deutsch.

Goodhart, C. A. E. (1984) *Monetary Theory and Practice: The UK Experience*,
London: Macmillan.

—— (1986) 'Financial innovation and monetary control', *Oxford Review of Economic
Policy* 2(4), Winter: 79–102.

Grabel, I, (1996) 'Financial markets, the state and economic development: controversies within theory and policy', *International Papers in Political Economy* 3(1).

Graziani, A. (1989) 'The theory of the monetary circuit', *Thames Papers in Political
Economy*, London: Thames Polytechnic.

Griffith-Jones, S. with Cailloux, J. and Pfaffenzeller, S. (1998) 'The East Asian financial crisis: a reflection on its causes, consequences and policy implications', *IDS
Discussion Paper* No. 367, Brighton: University of Sussex.

Hardwicke, Philip Yorke, Earl of (ed.) (1778) *Miscellaneous State Papers from 1501 to
1726*, London: W. Strahan and T. Cadell.

Hayek, F. A. (1935) *Prices and Production*, New York: Augustus M. Kelly.

Henwood, D., (1997) 'The stock market and the economy', *Review of Radical
Political Economy* 29(4), Fall: 144–8.

Hilferding, R. (1981) *Finance Capital: A Study of the Latest Phase of Capitalist Development*, edited and introduced by Tom Bottomore, translated by Morris Watnick and Sam Gordon, London: Routledge and Kegan Paul.

Hsieh, D. (1991) 'Chaos and non-linear dynamics: application to financial markets', *Journal of Finance* 46(5): December 1839–77.

Hyndman, H. M. (1932) *Commercial Crises of the Nineteenth Century*, with a new preface by John A. Hobson, Reprints of Economics Classics, New York: Augustus M. Kelly Publishers, 1967.

Imperato, A. (1997) *Informazione Aspettative ed Incertezza*, Napoli: Edizione Scientifiche Italiane.

Juric, A. J. (1998) 'The contagion effect of the East Asian crisis on Eastern Europe', dissertation submitted for the degree of MA in European Studies, London: South Bank University.

Kaldor, N. (1982) *The Scourge of Monetarism*, Oxford: Oxford University Press.

Kalecki, M. (1937) 'The Principle of Increasing Risk', *Economica* 4, revised as 'Entrepreneurial capital and investment', in *Selected Essays on the Dynamics of the Capitalist Economy 1933–1970*, Cambridge: Cambridge University Press.

—— (1964) 'Econometric model and historical materialism', in *On Political Economy and Econometrics: Essays in Honour of Oskar Lange*, Warszawa: Polish Scientific Publishers.

—— (1971) 'Determinants of profits', in *Selected Essays on the Dynamics of the Capitalist Economy 1933–1970*, Cambridge: Cambridge University Press.

Keynes, J. M. (1930) *A Treatise on Money in Two Volumes. 1: The Pure Theory of Money*, London: Macmillan.

—— (1936) *The General Theory of Employment, Interest and Money*, London: Macmillan.

—— (1937) 'The general theory of employment', *Quarterly Journal of Economics* 51: 209–23.

—— (1939) 'Professor Tinbergen's method', *Economic Journal* 49, September: 552–68.

Kindelberger, C. P. (1989) *Manias, Panics and Crashes: A History of Financial Crises*, London: Macmillan.

—— (1993) *A Financial History of Western Europe*, Oxford: Oxford University Press.

—— (1996) *World Economic Primacy 1500–1990*, New York: Oxford University Press.

Kregel, J. A. (1995) 'Neoclassical price theory, institutions, and the evolution of securities market organization', *Economic Journal* 105, March: 459–70.

—— (1996) 'Some risks and implications of financial globalization for national policy autonomy', *UNCTAD Review*: 55–62.

—— (1996) *Origini e Sviluppo dei Mercati Finanziari*, Arezzo, Italy: Banca Popolare dell'Etruria e del Lazio/Studi e Ricerche.

Law, J. (1750) *Money and Trade Considered: With a Proposal for Supplying the Nation with Money*, Glasgow: R. & A. Foulis.

Luxemburg, R. (1951) *The Accumulation of Capital*, translated by Agnes Schwartzschild, London: Routledge and Kegan Paul.

Mabbett, D. (1997) 'Pension funding: economic imperative or political strategy?' *Discussion Paper Series No. 97/1*, Uxbridge: Department of Government, Brunel University.

Machlup, F. (1978) *Methodology of Economics and Other Social Sciences*, New York: Academic Press.

Magdoff, H. and Sweezy, P. M. (1997) *Stagnation and the Financial Explosion*, New York: Monthly Review Press.

Markowitz, H.M. (1952) 'Portfolio selection', *Journal of Finance* 7(1): 77–91.

—— (1959) *Portfolio Selection: Efficient Diversification of Investment*, New York: John Wiley.

—— (1990) *Mean-Variance Analysis in Portfolio Choice and Capital Markets*, Cambridge, MA: Basil Blackwell.

Marsh, P. (1990) *Short-termism on Trial*, London: Institutional Fund Managers' Association.

Marx, K. (1959) *Capital, Volume III: The Process of Capitalist Production as a Whole*, Moscow: Progress Publishers.

Minsky, H. P. (1975) *John Maynard Keynes*, New York: Columbia University Press.

—— (1978) 'The Financial Instability Hypothesis: a restatement', *Thames Papers in Political Economy*, London: Thames Polytechnic.

—— (1982) 'Debt-deflation processes in today's institutional environment', *Banca Nazionale del Lavoro Quarterly Review* 143, December.

—— (1986) *Stabilizing an Unstable Economy*, New Haven, CT: Yale University Press.

Morgenstern, O. (1963) *On the Accuracy of Economic Observations*, second edition, Princeton, NJ: Princeton University Press.

Mott, T. (1985) 'Towards a post-Keynesian formulation of liquidity preference', *Journal of Post-Keynesian Economics* 8, Winter 1985–1986.

Murphy, A.E. (1997) *John Law: Economic Theorist and Policy-maker*, Oxford: The Clarendon Press.

Organization for Economic Co-operation and Development (1996) 'Ageing in OECD countries: a critical policy challenge', *Social Policy Studies* 20, Paris: OECD.

—— (1995) *The New Financial Landscape*, Paris: OECD.

Pilbeam, K. (1998) *Finance and Financial Markets*, London: Macmillan.

Quinn, B. (1993) 'Derivatives – where next for supervisors?', *Bank of England Quarterly Bulletin* 33(4), November: 535–8.

Raines, J. P., and Leathers , C. G. (1998) 'Institutional characteristics in the formation of stock prices: the views of Veblen and Keynes', paper presented at the Annual Meeting of the History of Economics Society in Montreal, Canada, June.

Roll, R. and Ross, S. (1980) 'An empirical investigation of the arbitrage pricing theory', *Journal of Finance* 35(5), December: 1073–1103.

Rybczyński, T. M. (1988) 'Financial systems and industrial restructuring', *National Westminster Bank Quarterly Review*, November: 3–13.

Sawyer, M. C. (1985) *The Economics of Michał Kalecki*, London: Macmillan.

Shaw, E.S. (1973) *Financial Deepening in Economic Development*, New York: Oxford University Press.

Singh, A. (1997) 'Financial liberalization, stock markets and economic development', *The Economic Journal* 107(442), May: 771–82.

Smith, A. (1904) *An Inquiry into the Nature and Causes of the Wealth of Nations*, Oxford: Oxford University Press,

Steil, B. (1992) 'Regulatory foundations for global capital markets', *Finance and the International Economy: The Amex Bank Review Prize Essays* 6.

Steindl, J. (1945) *Small and Big Business: Economic Problems of the Size of Firms*, Oxford: Basil Blackwell.

—— (1976) *Maturity and Stagnation in American Capitalism*, New York: Monthly Review Press.

—— (1982) 'The role of household saving in the modern economy', *Banca Nazionale del Lavoro Quarterly Review* 140, March, reprinted in J. Steindl, *Economic Papers 1941–88*, London: Macmillan, 1990.

Streisler, E. (1969) 'Structural economic thought: on the significance of the Austrian School today', *Zeitschrift für Nationalökonomie* 29: 237–66.

Sweezy, P. M. (1958) 'Veblen on American capitalism', in D. E. Dowd (ed.) *Thorstein Veblen: A Critical Appraisal*, Ithaca, NY: Cornell University Press.

Tobin, J. (1969) 'A general equilibrium approach to monetary theory', *Journal of Money, Credit and Banking* 1(1), February: 322–38.

Toporowski, J. (1989) 'The financial system and capital accumulation in the 1980s', in F. Green (ed.) *The Restructuring of the UK Economy*, Hemel Hempstead: Harvester Wheatsheaf.

—— (1993) 'Profits in the UK economy during the 1980s', *Review of Political Economy* 5(1), January; 65–84

—— (1993) *The Economics of Financial Markets and the 1987 Crash*, Aldershot: Edward Elgar.

—— (1994) 'Banking and finance', in P. Arestis, P. and M. C. Sawyer (eds.) *The Elgar Companion to Radical Political Economy*, Aldershot: Edward Elgar.

—— (1994) 'Corporate liquidity, capital markets and their valuation', *Economie Appliquée* tome XLVI, no. 3: 65–84.

—— (1997) 'Financial fragility in the banking systems of transitional economies in Eastern Europe', in S. Sharma (ed.) *Restructuring Eastern Europe: The Microeconomics of the Transition Process*, Cheltenham: Edward Elgar.

—— (1998) 'Capital market inflation and privatisation in capitalist and post-communist economies', *Zagreb International Review of Economics and Business* 1(2): 77–89.

—— (forthcoming) 'European destiny and macroeconomic responsibility in the financial systems of Germany and the UK: a balance sheet approach', in S. Frowen (ed.) *Financial Competition, Risk and Responsibility*, London: Macmillan.

Veblen, T. (1904) *The Theory of Business Enterprise*, New York: Charles Scribner's Sons.

Veblen, T. (1921) 'The captains of finance and the engineers', in *The Engineers and the Price System*, reprinted in Wesley C. Mitchell (ed.) *What Veblen Taught: Selected Writings of Thorstein Veblen*, New York: The Viking Press, 1936.

Walras, L. (1954) *Elements of Pure Economics of the Theory of Social Wealth*, translated by William Jaffé, London: George Allen and Unwin.

World Bank (1989) *The World Development Report 1989*, New York: Oxford University Press for the World Bank.

—— (1994) *Averting the Old Age Crisis: Policies to Protect the Old and Promote Growth*, World Bank Policy Research Report, New York: Oxford University Press.

—— (1997) *Global Economic Prospects and Developing Countries*, Washington, DC: World Bank

Wray, L.R. (1994) 'The political economy of the current US financial crisis', *International Papers in Political Economy* 1(3).

Index